W9-BEU-091

Japan

Japan

BY RUTH BJORKLUND

Enchantment of the World™
Second Series

CHILDREN'S PRESS®

An Imprint of Scholastic Inc.

Frontispiece: **Ninna-ji Temple, Kyoto**

Consultant: Hiroko Kataoka, Professor, Asian and Asian American Studies, California State University, Long Beach
Please note: All statistics are as up-to-date as possible at the time of publication.

Book production by The Design Lab

Library of Congress Cataloging-in-Publication Data
Names: Bjorklund, Ruth, author.
Title: Japan / by Ruth Bjorklund.
Description: New York, NY : Children's Press, an imprint of Scholastic Inc.,
    2018. | Series: Enchantment of the world | Includes bibliographical
    references and index.
Identifiers: LCCN 2016052309 | ISBN 9780531235690 (library binding : alkaline
    paper)
Subjects: LCSH: Japan—Juvenile literature.
Classification: LCC DS806 .B523 2018 | DDC 952—dc23
LC record available at https://lccn.loc.gov/2016052309

1 2 3 4 5 6 7 8 9 10 R 27 26 25 24 23 22 21 20 19 18

Buddhist statues, Nikko National Park

Contents

CHAPTER 1   Under the Rising Sun **8**

CHAPTER 2   Islands in the Sea **14**

CHAPTER 3   Island Hopping **24**

CHAPTER 4   An Ancient and Modern Land **38**

CHAPTER 5   The Empire of Japan **60**

CHAPTER 6 Innovation and Efficiency 70

CHAPTER 7 National Pride 80

CHAPTER 8 The Spirit World 88

CHAPTER 9 Grace and Beauty............................. 98

CHAPTER 10 Work and Play 110

Timeline.................................128

Fast Facts 130

To Find Out More...........................134

Index 136

Left to right: **Tokyo, Steller's sea eagle, children at a festival, carp flags, fox statue**

CHAPTER 1

Under the Rising Sun

TOMOE RUSHED HOME FROM SCHOOL AND CHANGED out of her uniform. She looked over at her brother, Ren, who was reading, and said, "*Junbi wa dekita*," "Are you ready?" In Japanese, her question would be written like this: 準備はできた. The Japanese language is written using characters to represent words. Ren told his sister he was just finishing his homework and was looking forward to the big game.

The big game, for them and for many around Japan, was the opening day of the "Spring Koshien," one of two national high school baseball tournaments. Millions of fans around the country watch on television, and thousands fill the stands. This year, Ren and Tomoe's high school was invited to play in the tournament, which is an enormous honor. Both Tomoe and Ren played on their elementary school teams. Tomoe, who is named after a legendary woman *samurai* named Tomoe

Opposite: **Baseball is one of the most popular sports in Japan. As of 2017, teams from Japan had won the Little League World Series ten times.**

Gozen, continues to play sports in school. Samurai were sword-wielding warriors who protected the nobility and their castles and estates. Today, Tomoe Gozen is the subject of many novels, movies, video games, and manga and anime stories. Manga is the very popular form of comic book that originated in Japan. Anime is animated film based on Japanese manga. Manga and anime are created for people of all ages and feature stories of all kinds.

Japan is a nation of more than six thousand islands. Some are tropical islands with nearby coral reefs; others have mountain ranges covered in snow. Nearly all people live on just four of the islands. Most people live in cities, and the cities are crowded. People use trains to go everywhere. Japan has one of the most modern railway systems in the world. The country is well known for its "bullet trains," which reach speeds of more than 200 miles per hour (320 kilometers per hour). Japanese trains always run on time.

More than ever, Ren is looking forward to his family's annual summer vacation. This year they are going to Tokyo, Japan's capital city and one of the most populated and sophisticated cities in the world. From his hometown in Kyoto to Tokyo, his family will be taking two trains. Along the way, he will buy an *ekiben*, a delicious and decorative boxed lunch

Young people read manga comic books at a shop in Japan. About five hundred million manga books are sold in Japan every year. They account for roughly half of all the book sales in the nation.

The Shinjuku area of Tokyo is famed for its bright lights and busy streets.

sold at train stations. Ren and Tomoe's mother is an excellent cook. They look forward to the school lunches she makes each day. She carefully prepares and arranges their food in patterns and designs and puts them in a *bento* box, a special Japanese lunch box. There are national competitions for the cleverest bento box arrangements.

Tokyo will be an amazing adventure. The list of things to do is endless. There are thousands of manga shops alone, along with museums, shrines, and gardens. Ren is looking forward to seeing the robot science museum. Tomoe is eager to see the animation museum. In August, hundreds of *matsuri*, or festivals, take place around Japan. All the Shinto shrines will have parades, music, and dance. Shinto is an ancient Japanese religion. There will also be more than two hundred Obon festivals, the biggest Buddhist festival of the year. For three days during Obon, Japanese people gather to enjoy dancing, drumming, parades, and lanterns lit and floating at night in the rivers and harbors.

Ren and Tomoe's family will also visit Mount Fuji, the snowcapped volcano near Tokyo. Japan has thirty-one national parks. Some in the southern islands include beautiful beaches, while many northern parks have mountains, lakes, rivers, waterfalls, and hot springs, called *onsen*. If they have time, Ren and Tomoe's parents want to visit Nikko National Park. The park is home to the seventeenth-century Toshogu Shrine. It has classic Japanese architecture and dramatic *torii* gates. In Japan, there is always one more thing to see.

Kegon Falls in Nikko National Park attracts many thousands of visitors every year.

CHAPTER 2

Islands in the Sea

角島 2 Km
Tsunoshima

JAPAN IS AN ARCHIPELAGO, OR STRING OF ISLANDS. These islands were once part of a peninsula, but millions of years ago, they separated, becoming islands. Today, Japan is surrounded by the Pacific Ocean on the east, the Sea of Japan to the west, the Sea of Okhotsk to the north, and the East China Sea to the south. Its nearest neighbors are South Korea in the west and Russia to the north. The southern Japanese island of Tsushima is only 33 miles (53 km) from Pusan, South Korea. Farther west across the Sea of Japan lies North Korea and China.

Japan's archipelago stretches in a long, north–south arc for about 1,865 miles (3,000 km). With a total area of 145,914 square miles (377,915 sq km), Japan is slightly smaller than the U.S. state of California and is about the same size as Germany. The country is made up of 6,852 islands. Only 426 islands are inhabited, and nearly everyone lives on one of four islands—Honshu, Hokkaido, Kyushu, or Shikoku.

Opposite: **Bridges connect some of Japan's islands. The Tsunoshima Bridge crosses the Sea of Japan, connecting Tsunoshima to the large island of Honshu.**

Japan's Geographic Features

Area: 145,914 square miles (377,915 sq km)

Highest Elevation: Mount Fuji, 12,388 feet (3,776 m) above sea level

Lowest Elevation: Lake Hachiro, 13 feet (4 m) below sea level

Number of Islands: 6,852

Deepest Lake: Lake Tazawa, 1,388 feet (423 m)

Longest River: Shinano, 228 miles (367 km)

Average High Temperature: In Tokyo, 85°F (29°C) in July, 49°F (10°C) in January

Average Low Temperature: In Tokyo, 71°F (22°C) in July, 34°F (1°C) in January

Average Annual Precipitation: In Tokyo, 55 inches (140 cm)

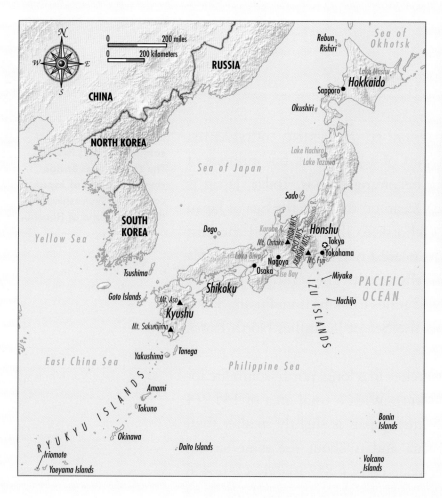

Mountains and Forests

Nearly 70 percent of Japan is covered in mountains, volcanoes, forests, or woodlands. A mountainous region on Honshu Island is known as the Japan Alps, with many peaks rising to more than 9,800 feet (3,000 meters). Three major mountain ranges occupy this area, Hida, Kiso, and Akaishi. The mountains are mostly granite rock with deep river gorges and valleys. Between this region and the capital city of Tokyo is snowcapped Mount Fuji, Japan's highest peak, rising 12,388 feet (3,776 m) above sea level. Nearly all of Japan's islands are mountainous. The island of Kyushu contains Mount Aso, rising 5,223 feet (1592 m) above sea level. It is one of the country's most active volcanoes and has one of the world's largest calderas, or volcanic craters. Most peaks there are covered in beech forests. Some mountains are heavily forested, and some are bare and rocky.

Steam rises from the lake that fills Aso Crater.

Protecting Nature

Japan has thirty-one national parks and many more protected areas. The nation's national parks protect a variety of environments, such as volcanoes, forests, marshes, beaches, rocky coastlines, and underwater marine caves and coral reefs. Some parks are near large populations, such as Nikko National Park outside of the capital city of Tokyo. Others are in isolated and unpopulated places such as Rishiri-Rebun-Sarobetsu National Park, which includes the vast Sarobetsu wetlands and the remote islands of Rishiri and Rebun. On Hokkaido, the largest of the northernmost islands, the mountains of Shiretoko National Park are rugged and remote. People who want to see the most remote areas of the park mostly do so by boat. The southernmost national park is Iriomote-Ishigaki National Park. The park covers several islands and the East China Sea. The islands have subtropical forests, mangrove swamps, sandy beaches, coral reefs, and turquoise water.

Ring of Fire

Japan sits on top of four tectonic plates, which are massive sections of Earth's outer layer. Hot melted rock, called magma, flows beneath the crust. Fault lines, or cracks in the plates, shift, strain, and slowly plow into each other. Many volcanoes rise near areas where tectonic plates meet. As the tectonic plates collide, the force pushes steam, gas, ash, and magma (called lava aboveground) up through the opening in a volcano.

Japan is part of a zone around the edge of the Pacific Ocean called the Ring of Fire. The area contains nearly 75 percent of the world's active volcanoes. Japan has hundreds

Volcanoes often erupt with some warning. Scientists keep watch on Japan's active volcanoes. Signs of a possible eruption include tremors (small earthquakes) and wisps of steam and smoke escaping from the mountaintop. Two volcanoes on the island of Kyushu—Aso and Sakurajima—have erupted in recent years. Lava spilled down their mountainsides, but no one was injured. However, on September 27, 2014, Mount Ontake on Honshu erupted.

Mount Ontake is near Mount Fuji and is usually crowded with visitors and hikers. The eruption came with little warning. Hundreds of people were on the slopes of the mountain when it exploded with steam, water, ash, lava, and toxic gases. More than fifty hikers died, and many others were injured by gas and falling rocks. The mountain continued to spew gas and rocks for several days in what was Japan's worst volcanic disaster in nearly a century.

of dormant or extinct volcanoes. However, there are also 110 active volcanoes in Japan, which is about 10 percent of all active volcanoes on Earth.

Earthquakes

Colliding tectonic plates cause earthquakes. More than one thousand earthquakes strike Japan each year. Most are magnitude 3 or less, which are mild and may go unnoticed. But several are above magnitude 5 each year. Not all of Japan's earthquakes occur on land. When earthquakes occur at sea, a tsunami, or a series of massive waves, sometimes results. In March 2011, the largest earthquake ever to hit Japan occurred offshore. It was measured as a magnitude 9 and shook for three to five minutes. There were thousands of aftershocks, smaller earthquakes following a large one. An hour after the earthquake struck, waves traveling 500 miles per hour (800 kph) hit the east coast of Honshu. In some areas, the waves were as high as 90 feet (27 m) and traveled inland nearly 6 miles (10 km). Nearly sixteen thousand people died, and many

Waves swept through Kamaishi during the tsunami of 2011. The earthquake and tsunami damaged or destroyed about a million buildings in Japan.

more were missing or injured. Houses, buildings, cars, trucks, and ships were tossed up and swept away. A crucial nuclear power plant was damaged, and dangerous radiation leaked into the air and the water. Five years later, 175,000 people had not returned to their communities.

Lake, River, and Sea

Swift-moving rivers are found throughout Japan. The headwaters of many of the rivers are found on steep mountains. The water races to the sea, carving deep gorges and wide valleys along the way. The Kurobe River begins its rapid flow from a height of 9,514 feet (2,900 m) down to the Sea of Japan. Flowing down the mountains, Japan's rivers form more than two thousand waterfalls. Japan's longest river is Shinano River, which flows through the center of Honshu for 228 miles (367 km) and empties into the Sea of Japan.

Japan also has thousands of lakes. Five lakes surround Mount Fuji alone. Lake Biwa is the largest lake in Japan. Located on Honshu, it is about 40 miles (64 km) long. Lake Mashu, a crater lake on Hokkaido, is one of the clearest lakes in the world.

The active magma beneath Japan warms water underground. The heated water is sometimes forced up to the surface in the form of hot springs. Aboveground, the hot springs form steaming pools of water, which are called *onsen*.

Lake Mashu in northern Japan is remarkably clear. It is often possible to see more than 100 feet (30 m) below the surface.

Climate

Japan has a temperate climate with four seasons. In spring, warm winds from China blow across the Sea of Japan, bringing an end to winter. Flowering trees bloom throughout the

Students walk through a downpour in Kyoto, where rain is common throughout the year.

country. But the warm weather can cause avalanches in the mountains as the snow melts. May to June is the start of the rainy season. By July, the temperatures can reach 95 degrees Fahrenheit (35 degrees Celsius), especially on the southern islands. August and September are stormy months. Typhoons, which are known as hurricanes in the Western Hemisphere, sometimes strike and cause great flooding and other damage. October and November are generally mild months. Many trees turn color from green to red, yellow, and orange. December brings the cold winds of winter. Much of the country near the Sea of Japan becomes blanketed in snow. The northern island of Hokkaido often has winter temperatures below freezing. The city of Sapporo is one of the snowiest cities in the world, with an average snowfall of 190 inches (485 centimeters).

Urban Landscape

Tokyo, the capital city, is located on the island of Honshu. It is heavily populated, with more than nine million people. Outside the city's core, settlement spreads so far that it merges with Yokohama, Japan's second-largest city. Yokohama has a population of 3,730,158, and is a leading commercial center and home to a major shipping port. Yokohama is also home to many museums, universities, and Japan's largest Chinatown. The city features formal public gardens, parks, shrines, theaters, and concert halls.

Osaka has a population of 2,702,455 and is Japan's third-largest city. It was once noted for its textiles but is now an important manufacturing hub with a major shipping port. It is also one of Japan's major banking and financial centers as well as a national center for news media and publishing. Osaka also has more than a dozen universities, many theaters, museums, and cultural centers.

Nagoya, with a population of 2,306,901, is an important industrial city on Ise Bay. It is a major transportation hub, with an airport, high-speed trains, highways, and a shipping port. From Nagoya, goods are easily shipped throughout the country and to the rest of the world. Nagoya was first established in 1610, when a great castle was built. The castle was destroyed by fire, but rebuilt in 1959. One of Japan's oldest Shinto shrines, Atsuta, is located in Nagoya.

Sapporo, with a population of 1,958,157 is Japan's fifth-largest city. It is a somewhat new city, established by the Japanese government in 1871. It is a commercial and publishing center, as well as a center for the logging industry. Sapporo is near many mountains. Winters bring heavy snow, and the area attracts skiers and others who enjoy winter sports. The city is a former host of the Winter Olympics.

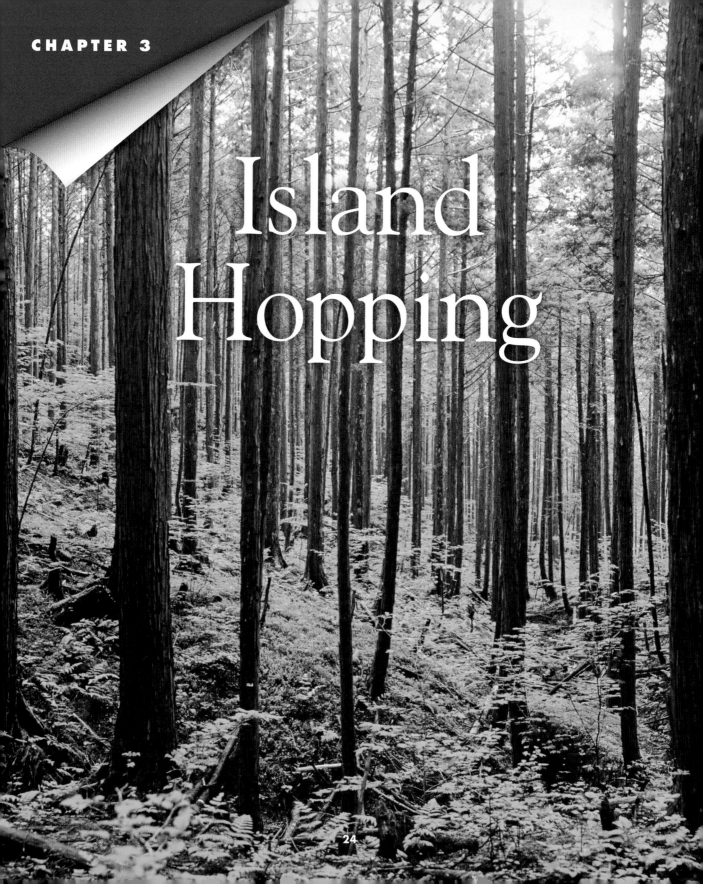

CHAPTER 3

Island Hopping

ON A VOYAGE FROM OKINAWA ISLAND, IN southern Japan, to Rebun Island, in northern Japan, a wide array of landscapes and wildlife will come into view. Japan's many plant and animal species are affected by the differences in weather and geography. Japan has subtropical islands where orchids grow and tropical fish dwell and subarctic islands that alpine trees and fur seals make their home.

Opposite: **A forest in central Japan. About 67 percent of the land in Japan is covered with forest, one of the highest percentages of any country in the world.**

Forests, Trees, and Flowers

There are more than four thousand plant species native to Japan. The range of temperatures paired with abundant rainfall allow a variety of plants and trees to thrive. Each climate zone shows differences in vegetation.

Satoyama

As long ago as 600 CE, Japan had cut down its timber forests for housing and fuel. Nobles built castles and farmers and villagers built cottages and burned wood for cooking and heating. By the 1500s, the population of Japan boomed. There were more than ten million people and the demand for timber grew. War broke out in 1570 and the army needed wood. After the war, cities grew quickly, nobles built more castles, and religious leaders built more shrines and temples. By 1670, there were more than thirty million Japanese and most of the old growth forests had been logged. Without trees to hold down the soil, the topsoil washed away, making it difficult to farm. There were floods and landslides and the countryside looked barren.

The Japanese recognized that something needed to be done. They began planting trees. Foresters, government officials, and local loggers developed new methods of planting and growing trees. They planted Japanese cedar and Japanese cypress between villages, cities, and wilderness areas. These tree plantations are known as *satoyama*. Although today Japan's population tops 125 million, the planted forests remain and thrive.

In the south, island groups such as the Yaeyama and Ryukyu are surrounded by turquoise water and coral reefs. Along many rivers and coastlines are thick mangrove swamps. Dense subtropical jungles of cedar, camphor, and evergreen oaks blanket most of the islands. Few forests were logged on Yakushima, so many of the island's Japanese cedars are ancient. In fact, one Japanese cedar is 53 feet (16 m) around and is believed by many experts to be as much as five thousand years old. The largest Japanese hardwood is the camphor tree. It grows up to 100 feet (30 m) and can spread as wide as it is tall. Oil from the camphor is used in cleaning products and as an ointment to treat pain from arthritis and chest colds. Numerous plants

Japan's white egret orchid gets its name from its resemblance to the egret, a graceful white bird. The beautiful flowers grow in marshy areas and on high mountain slopes.

and vines creep along the forest floor and thick mosses cling to trees.

Flowering plants abound on the southern islands. Among them are hibiscus, poinsettia, ginger, orchid, and lily. One of the more unusual flowers is known as the konjac. This dark purple lily rarely blooms, but when it does, it stinks of rotting meat. The odor attracts flies, which pollinate the plant.

South and central Japan are temperate zones. Forests there are mainly composed of broad-leafed trees such as evergreen oak and katsura. Katsura trees grow as high as 100 feet (30 m) and have heart-shaped leaves that bud red in spring and turn brilliant orange in fall. Great stands of giant timber bamboo also grow in the temperate zones. Bamboo is a grass,

In autumn, Japan's deciduous forests turn brilliant colors of yellow, orange, and red.

but it can grow 100 feet (30 m) tall and measure 8 inches (20 cm) around. Conifers, or cone-bearing trees, also grow in the temperate zones. These include cedar, pine, and cypress. Cool temperate forests in central and northern Honshu and southern Hokkaido contain deciduous trees—trees that lose their leaves in winter—such as beech and oak. Chrysanthemum flowers and Japanese cherry trees grow on hillsides.

Subalpine and subarctic temperature zones are found in the highlands of Honshu and most of Hokkaido. Forests there are a mix of deciduous and conifer trees, such as ash, oak, walnut, fir, pine, cedar, and spruce. In northern Hokkaido and

National Flower

There is no official national flower of Japan, but flowers are very important in Japanese life. The two flowers held in highest esteem are the chrysanthemum, called *kiku,* and the cherry blossom, called *sakura.*

In the early eighth century, the Japanese royal family became fascinated by the chrysanthemum and began using it in their official family seal. It remains the official seal of the royal family as well as of the Japanese government. The chrysanthemum is drawn with sixteen petals and appears on official documents such as passports.

Cherry trees grow on hillsides and gardens throughout Japan. They are considered a national treasure.

When they blossom in spring, it is cause for celebration. The entire country becomes awash in pink blossoms, but only for a brief two weeks. To the Japanese, cherry blossoms are a reminder that life is precious.

nearby islands such as Rebun and Rishiri, alpine cypress and cedar grow. Many delicate alpine flowers survive the short growing season, including the Siberian lily, the dogtooth violet, the Japanese rose, and the Rebun lady's slipper.

The Animal World

Just as vegetation varies from southern Japan to northern Japan, so does wildlife. When the islands of Japan broke away from the Asian mainland, animals were stranded on the islands and could not migrate. To this day, animal species that live on one island do not necessarily live on other islands. Additionally, many animal species are endemic to Japan, meaning that they live nowhere else in the world. Among them are the Japanese dormouse, the Japanese macaque, and the Japanese giant salamander.

Land Mammals

There are about 130 land mammal species in Japan. More mammals live in central and northern Japan than in the southern islands. Many animals that live on Hokkaido are related to animals in Siberia, in northern Russia. These include the Ezo brown bear, the Siberian sable, the Siberian flying squirrel, and the Sakhalin red fox. In the dense forests throughout Hokkaido, Honshu, Shikoku, and Kyushu live sika deer, wild boar, black bear, and serow. A serow is a furry, horned animal related to goats and sheep.

Sables have an excellent sense of smell, which they use to hunt hares and other small animals. The animals were once hunted extensively for their soft, silky fur.

Two of the more unusual Japanese mammals are the tanuki and the Japanese macaque. The tanuki, also known as the raccoon dog, closely resembles a raccoon, but is, in fact, a wild dog. Tanukis are omnivorous, meaning that they eat both plants and animals. Their prey includes frogs, fish, rodents, and birds. They are unique among wild dog species in that during severe snowstorms or periods when there is not enough food, they can hibernate. The Japanese macaque is sometimes called the snow monkey because it lives in northern Japan, where snowfall is common. No other primates, except humans, live as far north as the Japanese macaque. Japanese macaques live in large social groups, with as many as one hundred monkeys sharing the same territory.

A mother and baby Japanese macaque relax in the warmth of an onsen, or hot spring, on a cold day.

A type of macaque called a Yaku monkey is a native of Yakushima Island in southern Japan. It originally came to the island from the Asian mainland. The Yakushima deer is also a native of Yakushima, and it too came from the mainland. Both are much smaller than their mainland relatives. Years ago, when Yakushima Island was heavily logged, both animals were the target of hunters. Since logging has ended and the loggers are gone from the forest, the animals have plenty to eat and no predators to hunt them. Their numbers are rapidly expanding. Other mammals on Yakushima and nearby southern islands are mice, deer, rabbits, weasels, mongooses, and the Ryukyu flying fox.

Subtropical Japan is home to two endangered land mammals. The Iriomote wildcat is a small wildcat that lives only on the island of Iriomote. About the size of a housecat, it has long brown hair with bands of dark spots, and one single white spot on its back. The Iriomote wildcat hunts mostly at night, feeding on rats, squirrels, frogs, birds, and fish. It has webbed feet and is a good swimmer, both of which are unusual features for a cat. The Tsushima leopard cat lives only on the island of Tsushima. The leopard cat has a gold-colored coat with dark spots. It is very shy and lives along streams, in shiny-leaved forests, and in stands of bamboo. Both wildcats are losing their habitat to expanding human development.

Birds

More than six hundred species of birds can be found in Japan. Many are endemic, such as the Okinawa rail, Blakiston's fish-

owl, and the Japanese red-crested crane. Common birds found in central and northern Japan include thrushes, warblers, robins, jays, owls, hawks, and eagles. The Fuji-Hakone-Izu National Park, on Honshu, is home to many bird species. The park also includes Miyake Island, which is nicknamed Bird Island for its many rare birds, including the Japanese pygmy woodpecker.

Migratory birds breed in Siberia and other northern regions and come to Japan to spend the winter. Hundreds of species come to the marshes and plains of eastern Hokkaido. One of the more spectacular visitors is the whooper swan. The whooper swan is a large white swan with a black and yellow bill and a wingspan as wide as 7 feet (2 m). The whooper swan is so heavy that it cannot stand on its legs for long and must spend most of its time swimming while looking for food. Another heavyweight visitor to Hokkaido is the Steller's sea

Steller's sea eagles are powerful hunters. Their most common prey are large fish such as salmon and trout, which they snatch from shallow water, but they also sometimes feed on ducks and even seals.

Japanese red-crowned cranes are known for their enthusiastic dancing behavior. The birds mate for life.

eagle. It is one of the heaviest eagles in the world, weighing between 12 and 20 pounds (5 and 9 kilograms). Its wingspan can be as much as 7.5 feet (2.3 m).

In eastern Hokkaido is Kushiro Wetlands National Park. The park's streams, marshes, and ponds are home to thousands of resident and migratory birds. Thanks to the conservation efforts of the Japanese government in establishing the park, the Japanese red-crowned crane has been protected. By 1926, it was believed that the crane was extinct, but a few were found, and efforts were raised to protect the birds. Today, more than one thousand Japanese red-crowned cranes live on Hokkaido. They are Japan's largest bird.

Birds make their home south of Honshu as well. On Kyushu live hawks, cuckoos, kingfishers, woodpeckers, fly-

National Bird

The national bird of Japan is the Japanese green pheasant. It lives throughout much of the Japanese archipelago. The male of the species is one of the most colorful birds in the world. Males have dark green feathers, an iridescent violet-colored neck, a red face, and purple tail. They molt in late summer and go into hiding until their beautiful plumage regrows. Females are light brown with darker spots. Green pheasants feast on seeds, berries, ants, and maggots. Although they are hunted by other animals as well as by humans, their numbers remains high.

catchers, and pheasants, among others. Many birds on the southern islands are shorebirds and ducks, such as gulls, plovers, egrets, albatrosses, herons, ibises, and the endangered scaly-sided mergansers. The Okinawa rail is an endangered species endemic to the island of Okinawa. It is mostly flightless. It is a shy bird with a loud call. The female and the male sing together in duets during sunrise and sunset.

Reptiles and Insects

Reptiles are found both on land and in the sea throughout Japan. Box turtles and pond turtles are found in freshwater areas. In the subtropical water live many species of sea turtles. These turtles migrate across the oceans and come ashore to lay and bury their eggs in the sand. Many of the loggerhead turtles that lay eggs in Japan migrate back to Baja California, Mexico, to feed. Six of the seven of the world's sea turtle species are at risk. Many concerned Japanese conservationists

Brilliantly colored fish swim near the coral reef off Okinawa.

manage sea turtle protection programs such as keeping predators away from the buried eggs and watching over the baby turtles when they hatch and go out to sea.

Snakes are found on land and sea throughout Japan. There are many species of grass, blind, and rat snakes. Japan is also home to dangerous snakes, such as the white-banded wolf snake and the poisonous pit viper. Other venomous, or poisonous, snakes in Japan include the black-banded sea krait and the Okinawa coral snake. The black-banded sea krait is related to cobras and deadlier than vipers.

Throughout the country are thousands of species of insects, butterflies, and moths. The Japanese emperor butterfly is the national butterfly. The male butterfly has dark brown-green wings with brilliant purple-blue markings and white and gold spots.

Fish and Marine Life

A variety of fish species, such as trout, salmon, and carp, live in Japan's lakes. Few rivers have large fish populations because many of them have dams and concrete channels, which reduce the food supply.

However, Japan has abundant sea life. Fish found in marine waters off the coast of Japan include salmon, tuna, bonito, and mackerel. Brightly colored tropical fish swim along the coral reefs. Japan's waters also have many marine mammals, including dolphins, seals, and humpback and gray whales. The shy dugong, a relative of the manatee, weighs a hefty 1,000 pounds (450 kg) and lives in swamps.

On the ocean floor lives the tiny but extremely poisonous blue-ringed octopus. The waters are also home to shellfish such as clams, oysters, and crabs, including the largest land-living shellfish in the world, the Okinawa coconut crab.

Whaling

Japan has made a strong effort to protect its forests, animals, and waterways. But in one area of conservation, Japan is at odds with most of the rest of the world. Japan is one of the few countries that still carry out whale hunts. Whale meat was once a staple of the Japanese diet, but that is no longer the case. The International Whaling Commission banned whaling, but Japan continues the practice, stating that the whales taken are for scientific study. Many people do not believe this, however, and the conflict continues.

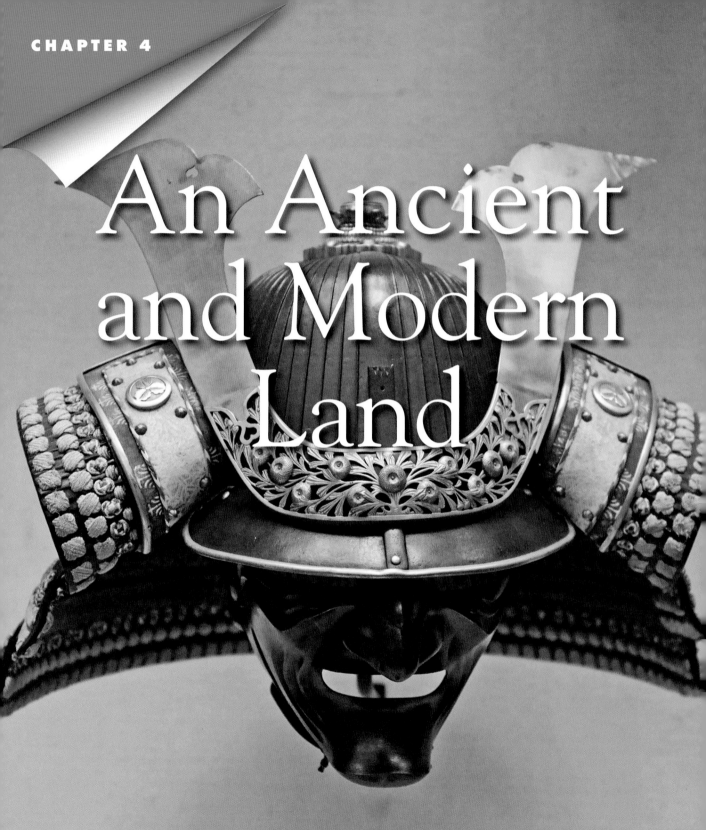

CHAPTER 4

An Ancient and Modern Land

AS MODERN AS JAPAN IS TODAY, SIGNS OF ITS ancient heritage are alive and very much present. In towns, cities, and even in the wilderness are traces of a former time. Ancient temples are preserved in downtown city parks. Crumbling shrines can be found along remote mountain trails. Traditions remain strong.

Prehistoric Japan

Early relatives of humans came to Japan about 370,000 years ago. The ancestors of today's Japanese people arrived between thirty-five thousand and thirty thousand years ago, after crossing a land bridge from the Asian mainland. They were hunters and gatherers. Japan had rich vegetation, fresh water, abundant seafood, and many birds and animals to hunt. Between 8000 BCE and 4000 BCE, Earth's climate warmed.

Opposite: **Elaborate helmets were a vital part of the armor of Japanese warriors called samurai.**

This Jomon figurine is at least 2,500 years old. Thousands of these Jomon figurines, called *dogu*, have been found in Japan.

Ice melted and seas rose. The rising water submerged the land bridges between the mainland and the Japanese islands. More fish came to the area, and with the warming, more vegetation grew. The population expanded.

Settling Down

The earliest known society in Japan is called the Jomon culture, which lasted from about 10,000 BCE to 300 BCE. During this time, people caught fish and gathered shellfish from the beaches. They hunted deer and wild boar. Archaeologists, scientists who study relics of the past, have found ancient pottery, stone tools, and signs that the people practiced some farming. By 300 BCE, more people made their way from the mainland, most settling on Kyushu. They became rice farmers who lived in small villages. The village way of life spread onto most islands, except for northern Honshu and Hokkaido. People stopped hunting and gathering and settled down to learn new skills and create close-knit communities.

The First Tenno

According to most records, Japan's monarchy has the longest unbroken line of descent in the world. Japanese legend has it that the first emperor, Jimmu, was a descendant of the sun goddess, Amaterasu. People believed emperors could speak with the gods. Jimmu and all his heirs to the imperial throne have held the title Tenno, Lord of Heaven. In ancient times, it was believed that the emperor had magical powers. It was not necessary for him to bother with day-to-day government. Since 660 BCE, when Jimmu was crowned, many imperial rulers have held a largely ceremonial role in Japanese life.

Changes in Society

Japanese farm communities became the core of everyday life. Clans, groups of extended family members, made up the communities. The idea that clans should have a ruling class of nobles took hold. Powerful clans joined ranks with other powerful clans. Many became wealthy serving the imperial government. The nobles managed the treasury, collected taxes, and oversaw farmland and food supplies.

Followers of the Buddhist religion came to Japan from Korea in the sixth century. Religious leaders formed another class of powerful people. They brought written language, which was previously unknown. The nobles hired the religious leaders to educate them. Once they could read, the nobles learned of civilizations beyond their own. Most of the new knowledge came from the writings of Chinese philosophers and political leaders.

In 749, Empress Koken took the throne. It was during her reign that Japan developed a powerful central government. It was based on the Chinese style of government, which was designed to have a head of state and a powerful council of advisers.

Devotion

In the mid-eighth century, Emperor Shomu and his wife, Empress Komyo, were curious about distant civilizations. They collected art such as paintings, sculptures, fabrics, pottery, paper crafts, and theater masks from China, Persia, and beyond. Their art collection has survived for more than 1,250 years.

By order of the emperor and empress, a giant statue of the Great Buddha was built in Nara as a prayer for peace in Japan and throughout the world.

One of the largest Buddha statues in the world, the Great Buddha is 63 feet (19 m) tall. The empress was responsible for building several Buddhist temples and convents. The largest convent is still active to this day, where nuns serve the blind. Taking her religious beliefs seriously, the empress built a bathhouse for the poor. It is said she vowed to "personally cleanse the bodies of one thousand people." When Emperor Shomu abdi-

cated his throne, he became a Buddhist priest. Empress Komyo, equally devout, became a Buddhist nun.

Rise of Military Rule

In 794, the Japanese capital moved to Kyoto. The model of central government held for another one hundred years, but the central government began to weaken because the nobles and religious leaders wanted greater control. The government granted both groups large estates. Farmers, who had been working on government-owned land and paying heavy taxes, abandoned the government fields and came to work for the new estates. The estate owners became more powerful and more competitive. The estates developed into self-governing regions, or provinces. They also developed private armies to defend their holdings. A class of skilled warriors, known as *samurai*,

A portrait of Minamoto Yoritomo from the 1100s. Yoritomo consolidated power to become the first shogun in 1192.

emerged. Many battles broke out between rival provinces.

After years of battles, a man named Minamoto Yoritomo came to power. He was given the title *shogun*, meaning military commander. He set up a central base far from the capital of Kyoto, in the city of Kamakura. There, he designed a new system of strict military government. In each province, he assigned one official to oversee the local military and another official to oversee land, farming, and taxes. During this period, nobles, priests, and their armies of samurai controlled most of the country. The system of military rule in Japan is known as a shogunate.

Change and Growth

During this period, advances in agriculture brought about an increase in the variety and quantity of food crops. This led to an increase in population, economic growth, and increased trade. A system of currency began to replace barter as a means of acquiring goods.

Although the country was expanding and developing, in time the military-style government weakened. Much of the cause lay with two invasions, in 1274 and 1281, by the Mongol army, which had gained control of China. The

A strong storm battered the ships of the Mongol army, preventing the Mongols from invading Japan.

Mongol leader, Kublai Khan, twice sent more than five hundred ships to attack Japan. The Japanese samurai were no match for the huge Mongol army. But during each invasion, typhoons struck, destroying the Mongols' ships and giving Japan the victory. Samurai warriors called the surprise storms *kamikaze*, meaning "divine wind."

Shogun Ashikaga Takauji moved the capital back to Kyoto. Takauji and his successors introduced changes that improved people's lives. New farming methods were developed, arts and crafts flourished, trade grew, and money was used to make purchases and exchanges easier. New social groups appeared. Whereas before there were the shoguns, nobles, priests, samurai, farmers, and peasants, now came a middle class of businesspeople, service workers, artisans, and merchants.

Peace and prosperity did not last. In 1441, the sixth shogun, Ashikaga Yoshinori, was assassinated. Military officers in the provinces refused to obey the central military government any longer. Battles broke out between rivals throughout Japan. The years 1467 through 1568 were so violent that historians refer to that era as the Age of Warring States.

Unity

In 1568, a leader named Oda Nobunaga was determined to unify Japan under a single ruler. His tactics were not peaceful, however. He conquered the city of Kyoto and rival provinces. His samurai burned down temples and shrines. He was later assassinated, but later shoguns continued his efforts to establish a central shogunate. By 1590, Nobunaga's successor,

The Imperial Palace in Edo. In 1600, around the time Edo became the capital, it was home to about sixty thousand people.

Toyotomi Hideyoshi, had seized most of the provinces and placed them under his control. He enacted a program known as a sword-hunt, intended to prevent revolt by farmers and other workers. People who chose not to be samurai had to give up their finely crafted swords, called *katana*. This was a difficult choice, since katanas provided them personal defense for their homes and property. But the status of a samurai was superior to that of a peasant or commoner, so they obeyed.

The Edo Period

In the early seventeenth century, the government moved to Edo, now called Tokyo. After Hideyoshi died, the emperor appointed Tokugawa Ieyasu shogun. The clan of Tokugawa held the position of shogun for 250 years. Tokugawa shoguns put Japan under strict control. They granted the most loyal nobles the largest and best parcels of land. The shogunate also closed the country to most foreign trade. Peace came to Japan under the Tokugawa shogunate, so the samurai had few battles to fight. Some chose to educate themselves, while others became soldiers for hire.

The Tokugawa shogunate developed close ties with the imperial family. It rebuilt castles and gave more landholdings to the emperors, empresses, and their families. The shogunate did more than rule the country, it also established rules for society. It believed in the teachings of Confucius, a sixth century BCE philosopher. The philosophy emphasized the importance of morals, education, and a class system. The shogunate imposed a strict social class system, with the emperor at the top. Below him was the shogun, nobles, samurai, farmers, artisans, merchants, and, lastly, outcasts. People were expected to show respect, accept arranged marriages, and dress according to their social class. People could not change their social class.

Beginnings and Endings

The Tokugawa shogunate ruled during a time of change. The shogunate built roads and highways. Farms increased production, more goods were manufactured, and markets grew. Arts and crafts flourished, as well as theater, music, puppetry, opera, poetry, and literature. Yet outside forces would lead to the powerful shogunate's decline. The samurai were increasingly angered by their circumstances. As in earlier times, they were paid with rice. But the economy had changed, and more people traded with money. As trade increased, merchants and businesspeople became wealthy and more powerful. They no longer wanted to follow the rules of the social order. The government raised taxes, and many people revolted. Loyalty to the shogunate dwindled.

At the end of the eighteenth century, Russia and other countries tried to trade with Japan, but the shogunate turned them away. Meanwhile, the Industrial Revolution was making great advances in many Western nations. Goods were being made easier, faster, and cheaper than ever before. The Western nations, especially the United States and Great Britain, wanted to expand their markets. Many nations had their eye on establishing trade with Japan, but the shogunate and the emperor continued to refuse such proposals. By the mid-nineteenth century, the United States had active trade with the Philippines, Guam, and the Kingdom of Hawaii. Trade had become even more efficient with the invention of steamships. No longer did ocean voyages rely on wind. The new ships burned coal as fuel, and they needed a harbor where they could take on provisions and refuel. Japan was the ideal location.

In 1853, U.S. president Millard Fillmore dispatched Commodore Matthew Perry of the U.S. Navy to approach the Japanese emperor. On July 8, 1853, Perry sailed four ships into Tokyo harbor. The ships were an unwelcome and disturbing sight. Commodore Perry stepped ashore and requested a meeting with the emperor. The Japanese officials refused, but

Perry insisted. The officials eventually accepted a letter from Fillmore. In February of the following year, Perry returned with a larger squadron of ships. The emperor and the shogunate agreed to meet Fillmore's requests. The agreement, called the Treaty of Kanagawa, was signed. The Japanese government promised that American ships would be protected while at anchor in Japanese harbors. Although the Americans were allowed to anchor in only two harbors, most of the treaty was otherwise balanced in favor of the Americans.

In the 1860s, several noble groups wanted to overthrow the shogunate and return power to the emperor, Komei. The leaders of two of the most important groups forced the shogun to leave Edo and meet with the emperor in Kyoto. En route, their convoy of ships crossed paths with British merchant ships. Foreign ships were not allowed in Japanese territorial

Commodore Matthew Perry and his troops came ashore at Yokohama in 1854 to sign the Treaty of Kanagawa. The tree depicted on the right still stands at the site.

waters when the Japanese were sailing on official business. The British were not informed, and a skirmish erupted. The British demanded payment for the attack. Meanwhile, the emperor banned all foreigners from Japan. Although many foreigners backed the shogunate, eventually the last shogun gave up control to the emperor. On February 3, 1867, the day Komei died, his fifteen-year old son Mutsuhito was crowned emperor. He became known as Emperor Meiji.

Emperor Meiji

By 1868, the shogunate had fallen, and the emperor was restored to power as supreme ruler. Emperor Meiji moved the court to Edo and changed its name to Tokyo, which means "eastern capital." His advisers were young and well educated. They changed Japan's style of government and in 1889 wrote the first constitution. They also made social reforms and

Japanese workers at machines in a silk factory in 1890. Textile manufacturing flourished in Japan in the late 1800s.

The First Modern Emperor

On February 3, 1867, at age fifteen, Mutsuhito was crowned the 122nd emperor of Japan. He would later become known as Emperor Meiji. The emperor's childhood had been spent in the era of the powerful Tokugawa shogunate. At this time, Japan was isolated from much of the world. But as the shogunate weakened, many young and educated government officials wanted Western-style modernization. The young emperor was an eager student of government and philosophy. He was especially fond of U.S. president Abraham Lincoln. Once Mutsuhito became emperor, he and many like-minded advisers began charting a new course for Japan.

In 1868, Emperor Meiji set out a Charter Oath of Five Principals. The charter was designed to encourage political and social reform. It included an elected legislature, equality among social classes, civil rights, freedom of choice, and banishment of the "evil customs of the past."

Emperor Meiji believed in a central government. He created a parliament and a system of cabinet ministers. He enacted land reforms, taking control from the nobles and allowed workers to own land. He established a ministry of education. Traditionally, only children of the nobility went to school. During his reign, thousands of public schools were built, and by 1905, more than 90 percent of girls and boys attended grade school. The emperor wanted a "rich country with a powerful army." He did away with the powerful samurai class and created a hired army. Meiji also pursued industrialization. Many factories, especially textile factories, were built during his reign. When the first railroad line was completed, he made a rare public appearance, symbolizing a new relationship between the imperial government and progress for the people.

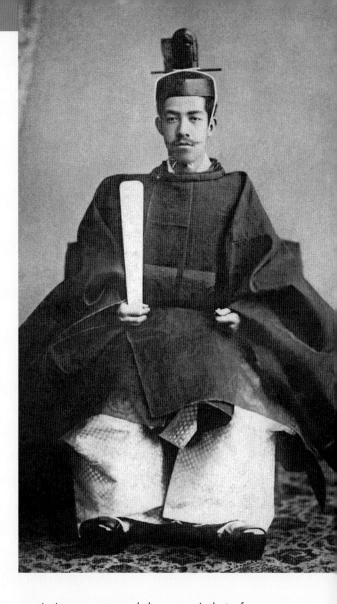

As Japan progressed, the country's desire for expansion grew. Emperor Meiji was the commander of the army and navy when Japan declared war on China and later Russia. The Meiji period pulled Japan out of a past dominated by tradition, but it also launched Japan into a chaotic future. Despite the wars that followed Meiji's reign, he left behind a strong legacy of a constitution, an elected government, a system of public education, and improvements in human rights.

allowed greater religious freedom. Technology, weaponry, manufacturing, and scientific invention were highly valued. Meiji's reign saw rapid expansion and modernization.

During the Meiji period, Japan sought wealth, military power, and respect from other nations. To press forward with its goals of developing a modern military and increasing factory output, Japan needed oil, coal, and steel. The island nation had to look beyond its borders for the raw materials it needed.

Japan began expanding into other countries. Korea was one of the first. It, too, had closed its doors to trade with foreign countries, but Japan convinced Korea to sign a trade treaty. This angered China, which considered Korea its territory. Both China and Japan established military bases in Korea. China assassinated Korea's pro-Japanese king, and in retaliation, Japan sunk Chinese warships. China and Japan officially declared war in 1894. Japan had a smaller army than China but more advanced weapons. Japan won the war in 1895 and occupied Korea until 1945.

Germany, France, and Russia pressed Japan to withdraw from Korea. Rather than retreat, Japan tightened its hold on Korea. The Europeans were enraged. Russia pushed the hardest, and in 1904, Japan and Russia (aided by Germany) went to war. It was another opportunity for Japan to show off its military might. In 1906, Japan shocked Western nations by defeating Russia, becoming the first Asian nation to conquer a European country. At last, Japan had earned the respect of the Western world.

Between Two Wars

Japan continued to expand its possessions, including acquiring important shipping ports in China. In 1914, World War I started in Europe, and it spilled over into Asia. Japan, siding with Great Britain and its allies, was responsible for guarding the West Pacific and the Indian Ocean against the German navy. After the war, Japan was granted Germany's holdings in the Pacific, including Micronesia and the Marshall Islands. Japan's economy boomed.

Looking for greater expansion, Japan invaded Manchuria, a region in northeastern China, in 1931. Soon, Japan returned to a policy of isolation; that is, separating itself from other countries. Instead of cooperating with Western powers, Japan began imitating them by colonizing other, weaker countries. Japan fought a brutal battle over Nanjing in China and Burma (now known as Myanmar). It occupied French Indochina—Vietnam, Cambodia, Laos—and the Dutch East Indies. These countries were an important part of Japan's supply route for goods, food, and oil. Japan imported most of its oil from the United States, but it feared that it would soon be shut out. As Japan continued its aggres-

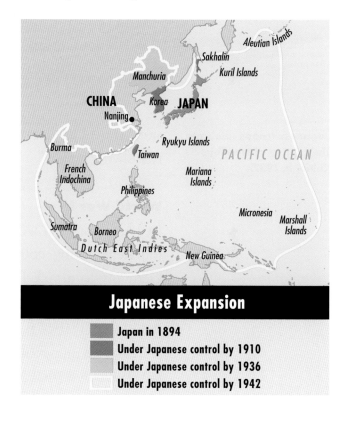

Japanese Expansion

Japan in 1894
Under Japanese control by 1910
Under Japanese control by 1936
Under Japanese control by 1942

Japanese troops celebrate the capture of Nanjing, China, in 1937.

sion, the United States placed sanctions, ending most U.S. trade with Japan.

World War II

In 1939, a second world war began as Germany started invading neighboring countries. Japan's military leaders expected Germany to attack European colonies and territories in Asia next. Japanese officials knew the Europeans would defend their holdings and they felt threatened. In 1940, despite its dislike and distrust of Germany's leader, Adolf Hitler, the Japanese government signed a treaty, called the Tripartite Act, with Germany and its ally, Italy. Each agreed to defend one another against any new attack from Great Britain, the United States, the Soviet Union (formerly Russia), and their allies.

Japan's Emperor Hirohito was commander in chief of the armed forces. In 1941, Japanese general Hideki Tojo came to

The Code of the Samurai

The code of ethics of the samurai is called Bushido, meaning "way of the warrior." The teachings of Buddhism and Confucius influenced the warrior's code. The seven moral principles of Bushido are rectitude (a sense of right and wrong, or conscience), courage, benevolence (caring for others), honor, respect, honesty, and loyalty. Three other principals are sometimes added: filial piety (respect for parents, grandparents, ancestors), wisdom, and care for the aged.

The samurai pledged complete loyalty to their military leader. Should their leader die in battle, the samurai pledged to seek revenge. There were several levels of samurai. For example, during the Meiji period, more than two million people were samurai. During World War II, the code of loyalty to Japan and to the emperor remained strong. The strongest followers of Bushido were

called kamikaze pilots—soldiers who volunteered to fly their warplanes into battleships and other military targets in suicide attacks, although many of these pilots were forced to fly. Today, formal Bushido rituals are practiced mostly in the martial arts and sumo wrestling.

power. Together they increased their control over China and French Indochina. The United States shut down oil exports to Japan and demanded that Japan pull its troops out of China, Indochina, and Burma. The negotiations reached a stalemate.

Then, on December 7, 1941, hundreds of Japanese fighter planes and bombers made a surprise attack on the U.S. naval base in Pearl Harbor, on the island of Oahu, Hawaii. In just two hours, the base was destroyed. The day after the attack, U.S. president Franklin Roosevelt declared war on Japan. In a short, blazing speech before Congress, he called the attack "a date which will live in infamy."

During the war, Japan gained control of most of East and Southeast Asia, as well as the western Pacific. The battles

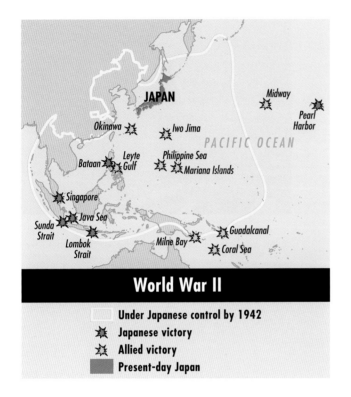

JAPAN

Midway

Pearl
Harbor

Okinawa

Iwo Jima

PACIFIC OCEAN

Leyte
Bataan Gulf

Philippine Sea

Mariana Islands

Singapore

Java Sea

Sunda
Strait

Lombok
Strait

Milne Bay

Guadalcanal

Coral Sea

World War II

☐ Under Japanese control by 1942
✷ Japanese victory
✷ Allied victory
■ Present-day Japan

between the United States and Japan in the Pacific were exceptionally bloody and brutal. Battles raged at sea, in the air, in jungles, cities, and remote hillsides. The United States bombed civilians and destroyed many Japanese cities. Eventually, the United States put Japan on the defensive and made more than one hundred air raids near Tokyo. Yet, Hirohito and his military commanders refused to surrender, because surrendering would mean unbearable humiliation.

Then, on August 6, 1945, the United States dropped the first atomic bomb on the city of Hiroshima. The bomb's destruction was unlike any other. Roughly two hundred thousand people eventually lost their lives and the city was left in shambles. Still, Japan did not surrender. On August 9, 1945, the United States dropped another atomic bomb, this time on Nagasaki. At ground zero where the bomb exploded, temperatures reached as high as 7,230°F (4,000°C). About seventy-four thousand people were killed instantly. Many more were injured, most later dying of the effects of the bomb's deadly radioactive fallout. On August 15, 1945, Hirohito announced Japan's surrender in a radio broadcast. No one other than the imperial family and his closest friends and advisers had ever heard his voice before.

Postwar Japan

The surrender brought humiliation and punishment. Great Britain, the Soviet Union, and China formed a council to assist the United States' occupation of Japan. The council had four goals—to punish Japan, rebuild its economy, form a democratic government, and eventually sign a peace treaty and build an alliance. The council punished Japan by taking away its colonies and disbanding its military. It reduced the position of emperor to a ceremonial role and placed more power in the hands of an elected government. The U.S. commander Douglas MacArthur ordered land and tax reforms. MacArthur drafted a new constitution that gave citizens, especially women, more rights and took away Japan's right to wage war. The United States occupied Japan until the signing of the San Francisco Peace Treaty in 1951. The island of Okinawa, the site of a large U.S. military base, remained under U.S. control until 1972. The U.S. military base remains there to this day.

The atomic bomb dropped on Hiroshima in 1945 flattened almost all of the city.

Jeeps move down an assembly line at a Mitsubishi factory in 1965. Japan has been one of the world's top car manufacturing nations since the 1960s.

Modern Japan

In the years after the war, the Japanese turned to building a new, modern country. With the help of the United States, Japan developed rapidly. Manufacturers who had once built military vehicles and weapons converted their technology and machinery into factories making peacetime goods. Machine gun factories started making sewing machines. Well-known companies such as Toyota and Nissan had built jeeps, tanks, ships, and warplanes. After the war, they designed and built fuel-efficient cars and trucks. Factories that made glass lenses for gunsights and periscopes began making binoculars and cameras. The man who would go on to start Sony had a company that made devices that sent signals from battleships, submarines, and warplanes. After the war, Sony factories began making radios, stereos, and televisions. Soon, Japan's products were being sold around the world.

Japan built modern railways, telecommunication systems, highways, and airports. It upgraded its harbors to allow large ships to anchor and load and unload goods. Japan built hydro-electric dams and nuclear power plants to provide electricity.

From the 1950s to the early 1990s, Japan became one of the most prosperous countries in the world. But in the early 1990s, the economies of many Western countries, as well as Japan's, were expanding too quickly. A financial crash came, and Japan was hit hard. Both companies and families lost a lot of money. For decades, Japan's economy had relied on selling goods to the rest of the world. But other countries, such as Korea and China, started making products more cheaply than Japan.

The Japanese people had to take on the challenge of rebuilding the economy again. They were making solid progress until 2011, when a disastrous earthquake and tsunami struck, killing more than fifteen thousand people and destroying a wide swath of the Honshu coast. A nuclear power plant in Fukushima was severely damaged and was shut down. Japan temporarily shut down all nuclear power plants and was forced to import expensive oil and gas to provide electricity. But without delay, the Japanese began cleaning up the wreckage. They rebuilt houses, hospitals, businesses, roads, railways, and bridges. They completed a massive seawall to protect the area from another tsunami. Regardless of what setbacks it may face, Japan continues to push forward, building a better future.

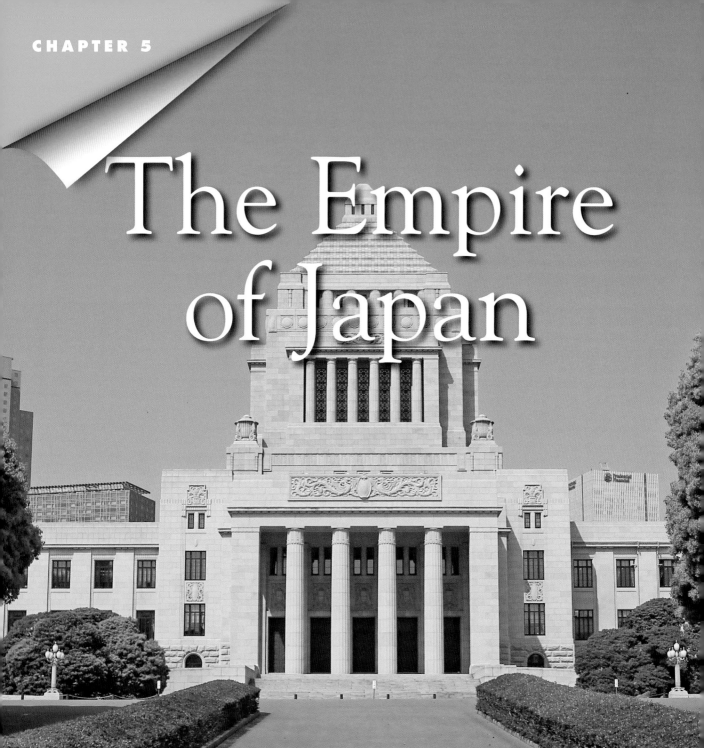

CHAPTER 5

The Empire of Japan

J APAN IS A CONSTITUTIONAL MONARCHY WITH A
parliamentary government. It has the oldest hereditary monarchy in the world, and one of the oldest parliaments. Japan's
monarchy has been in place for more than 2,600 years.

Opposite: **Japan's parliament building was completed in 1936.**

The Constitution
After World War II, U.S. commander Douglas MacArthur
drafted a new constitution for Japan, modeled after the
U.S. Constitution. The new constitution, adopted in 1947,

described three branches of government: executive, legislative, and judicial. It removed power from the emperor and gave it to the people to elect their leaders. Additionally, the new constitution guaranteed all citizens the right to individual freedoms, as well as equality under the law for both men and women. It also granted women the right to vote. The constitution states that Japan must be a peaceful nation and cannot wage war.

The Head of State

The emperor of Japan is the head of state. According to the constitution, he is the "symbol of the State and of the unity of the people," but has "no powers related to government." The emperor interacts with foreign dignitaries and performs ceremonial duties.

The emperor and the imperial family are subject to laws in the constitution called the Imperial Household Laws. One controversial part of the law is that women are not allowed to become emperor. Japan has had eight ruling empresses;

Emperor Akihito ascended to the Chrysanthemum Throne in 1989, after the death of his father, Hirohito. Akihito named his reign the Heisei period, meaning "achieving peace." Akihito was the first emperor to marry a commoner, Michiko Shoda. As a couple, they traveled around the world to show that Japan had remade itself into a peaceful and prosperous nation. The emperor has visited China, the United States, the South Pacific, and Pearl Harbor. In each visit, he paid his respects to those who died in battle and their families.

When a devastating earthquake and tsunami struck in 2011, Akihito made the first television broadcast by an emperor. He asked the Japanese "to work hand in hand, treating each other with compassion, in order to overcome these trying times." The catastrophe had damaged a nuclear power plant, leaving many people without electricity. Akihito asked the country to conserve electricity, and he ordered the imperial palace to do the same. Although he lacks power in the government, Akihito has shown Japan and the world true leadership.

The Sun Disk

The Japanese flag is known as the Hinomaru, meaning the "sun disk." The flag is a solid red circle on a field of white. The red circle represents the sun and the sun goddess, Amaterasu, who is considered the founder of Japan. White symbolizes the purity and honesty of the Japanese people. The origin of the flag is unknown, but records show it was used as far back as the seventh century. Later, it was carried into battle against the Mongol invasion in the thirteenth century and during the Warring States period in the fifteenth and sixteenth centuries. During the Meiji period, the emperor ordered that the flag be flown on Japanese merchant ships and naval vessels.

the last stepped down in 1770. But the constitution of 1889 banned women from inheriting the throne. Many in Japan today would like to remove the ban. Emperor Akihito's son, Crown Prince Naruhito, has only one child, a girl named Princess Aiko. If the constitution is not amended, Princess Aiko's male cousin will inherit the throne.

Executive Branch

The executive branch is made up of the prime minister and a cabinet of ministers. The prime minister is the head of government. Parliament chooses the prime minister and the prime minister appoints the cabinet ministers. Most ministers are members of parliament. Each minister oversees a different part of the government, such as justice, environment, and foreign affairs.

Legislative Branch

Japan's parliament, or legislative branch, is called the Diet. It is made of two houses. The most powerful house is the House of Representatives, which has 475 members elected to four-year terms. They decide important matters such as treaties and the budget. The House of Representatives also chooses the

A Japanese woman drops her ballot in a box during a recent election. Japanese people must be at least eighteen years old to vote.

prime minister from among its members. If the representatives are dissatisfied with the government, they can call for a new election. The prime minister can also call for a new election. This happens often, and most representatives' terms are two to three years.

The other house is called the House of Councillors. There are 242 councillors and each serves a full six-year term. The prime minister cannot call for a new election in the House of Councillors.

Japanese prime minister Shinzo Abe answers questions during a debate in the Diet.

Members of the Diet do not write laws. Cabinet ministers, experts, and other members of the administration discuss and propose new laws. The two houses study the proposals and vote whether or not to approve them.

Japan's National Government

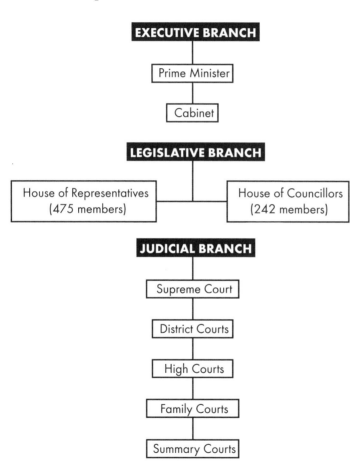

EXECUTIVE BRANCH

Prime Minister

Cabinet

LEGISLATIVE BRANCH

House of Representatives (475 members)

House of Councillors (242 members)

JUDICIAL BRANCH

Supreme Court

District Courts

High Courts

Family Courts

Summary Courts

Governing Tokyo

In 2016, Yuriko Koike was elected the first woman governor of Tokyo, the capital of Japan. Japan has far fewer women in government and business than Western countries do. Koike, however, won in a landslide. She is a former television news anchor who graduated from the Cairo University and speaks fluent Arabic. She is also Japan's former minister of defense and minister of environment.

After her election, she promised to "promote urban development while giving consideration to the environment." Besides governing the most densely populated city in the world, Koike's first years in office have included managing billions of dollars to prepare Tokyo to host the 2020 Olympic Games. Many believe the governor will open more doors for women in government and the workplace.

Judicial Branch

The highest court in Japan is the Supreme Court, which is made up of a chief justice and fourteen other justices. Justices are appointed by the cabinet. Other Japanese courts include district courts, high courts, family courts, and summary courts. Most cases are tried in district courts. Japan also has a lay judge system. Since May 2009, many district court cases are tried by three judges and six randomly chosen citizen-judges. The citizens investigate and ask questions before making a ruling.

Tokyo, the Capital

Tokyo was once a small fishing village called Edo. It later became a large estate surrounded by samurai forts. The Tokugawa shogunate took over the estate and built a castle. When Emperor Meiji came to power, he moved the government to Edo and renamed the city Tokyo. Today, Tokyo is one of the most populated cities in the world, with a population of 9,390,048. Its metropolitan area, meaning all the neighborhoods immediately surrounding the city, has a population of more than 13.6 million people. More than two million people commute into the city to work each day.

Besides being the nation's capital, Tokyo is the cultural and commercial center of Japan. Tokyo is fast-paced and crowded. Yet it is an orderly city with wide streets and both modern and historic buildings. The city is ablaze with color, from the pink cherry blossoms to the bright neon lights on buildings.

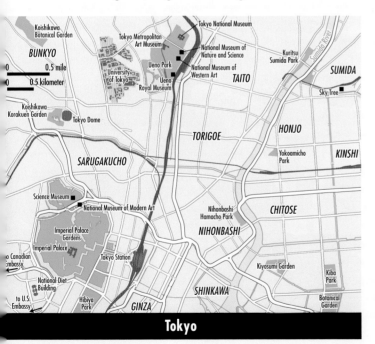

Tokyo

Tokyo has many diverse neighborhoods. The Ginza was Tokyo's first modern neighborhood. It is a world-famous shopping district, with luxury stores, nightclubs, restaurants, and art galleries. In the center of the city, surrounded by a moat, is the Imperial Palace and its vast, elegant gardens. The National Diet building and other government buildings are located nearby. Also in the city center are the National Museum of Modern Art and many other museums, including a science museum and a Japanese sword museum. Ueno Park is the city's largest park, with forest trails, gardens, Buddhist temples, Shinto shrines, a lake, and a zoo. Nearby, the Tokyo National Museum has a vast collection of ancient art and crafts, including pottery, sculptures, textiles, and paintings.

CHAPTER 6

Innovation and Efficiency

FOR CENTURIES, THE PEOPLE OF JAPAN RELIED ONLY on themselves. They grew what they ate, and made what they needed. But since the mid-nineteenth century, Japan has burst forth with invention and hard work to become a world leader in industry and commerce.

Opposite: **A Japanese farmer uses a tractor to plant young rice shoots in a flooded field.**

Agriculture

Japanese farmers are very productive. With just 12 percent of the land usable for farming, they are able to produce about 40 percent of the nation's food. Rice is the staple. After the rainy season, fields and hillsides turn a lush green as new shoots of rice begin to grow. Other crops grown in Japan include vegetables such as potatoes, cabbages, radishes, tomatoes, and onions; fruits such as apples, Japanese pears, Mandarin oranges, and

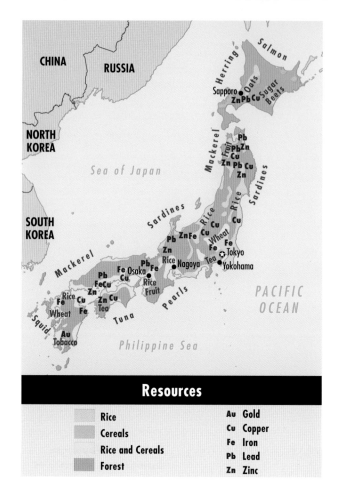

Resources

	Rice	**Au**	Gold
	Cereals	**Cu**	Copper
	Rice and Cereals	**Fe**	Iron
	Forest	**Pb**	Lead
		Zn	Zinc

watermelons; grains such as wheat and barley; and tea.

Meat and dairy products were not traditionally part of the Japanese diet. But tastes have changed. Japan imports most of its meat because there is little land available to raise livestock.

Fishing

Japan has one of the richest fisheries in the world. Fishers catch a wide variety, including tuna, mackerel, sardines, salmon, and flounder. Shellfish are also abundant. There are crabs, mussels, clams, and oysters. Octopus,

Bluefin Tuna Supply and Demand

Bluefin tuna is exceptionally prized in Japan. The nation accounts for about 80 percent of the world's consumption of the fish. Bluefin tuna is a large, fatty fish used in sushi and sashimi, two popular foods. It is so highly regarded, that sometimes price is no object. In 2013, a 500-pound (227 kg) tuna was sold for a record $1.7 million. But a result of bluefin's popularity is that too many fish are being killed off before they can reproduce or grow to full size. In 2015, Japan cut the amount allowed to be caught in half. It is hoped this will help bluefin tuna once again become abundant in Japan's waters.

Pearls were once regarded as a priceless gem, worn only by royals and the rich. Pearls grow inside oysters, and only by chance. A perfectly round natural pearl is extremely rare. Pearls are formed when a piece of shell or other debris gets inside an oyster's shell. The debris irritates the oyster's soft body. So, the oyster secretes a protective substance around the irritant which hardens into a pearl. In the late 1800s, a man named Mikimoto Kokichi, the son of a Japanese noodle maker, discovered a way to make oysters form perfectly round pearls. Using a needle, he placed a piece of mussel shell inside an oyster, forcing it to form a pearl. His method created a huge new industry for Japan. Oyster beds, or farms, flourished, especially along the coastline of the island of Shikoku. Each year, Japan produces about 20,000 tons of cultured pearls.

eel, squid, shrimp, seaweed, and kelp are all highly desired. To meet the high demand for seafood, Japanese fishing fleets also fish in distant waters.

Aquaculture, or fish farming, is another method Japan hopes will keep up with the demand for seafood. Farmed fish are fed in large underwater pens before being harvested for food.

Natural Resources

Japan has few natural resources. Most of the raw materials the country needs are imported. Three hundred years ago, Japan had logged most of its trees, so the country reforested by replanting trees. Not until the 1920s were Japan's forests somewhat healthy again. Today, nearly 40 percent of Japan's forests are tree farms. Japan still relies on imports to supply paper and building materials.

The nation has very few mineral resources. It once was a leading supplier of copper, but the copper mines have closed. Small amounts of other minerals are still mined, including iron, lead, zinc, iodine, and silica.

What Japan Grows, Makes, and Mines

AGRICULTURE (2014)

Rice	8,439,000 metric tons
Potatoes	2,456,000 metric tons
Mandarin oranges	875,000 metric tons

MANUFACTURING (VALUE, 2014)

Automaking	$546 billion
Chemical products	$255 billion
Food processing	$236 billion

MINING

Gypsum (2013)	5,500,000,000 metric tons
Silica (2012)	3,200,000,000 metric tons
Iodine (2013)	9,400 metric tons

Services

Nearly 70 percent of Japanese workers are employed in service industries. Service jobs are jobs that people do for each other. They include teachers, firefighters, bankers, bus drivers, government workers, and lawyers. People who work in stores,

Young women in traditional clothing pose for a Western tourist at a temple in Kyoto. About twenty million foreign visitors travel to Japan each year. Kyoto, a historic city that contains two thousand temples and shrines, is among the most popular tourist destinations.

restaurants, and hotels also work in service industries. The service industry is the fastest growing part of the economy.

Tourism is a major service industry. Japan is a popular tourist destination. People visit Tokyo and other cities such as Kyoto and Osaka to enjoy shopping, restaurants, theater performances, and museums. Tourists also visit shrines and temples, such as the Golden Pavilion or Himeji Castle. Others visit to enjoy the outdoors. They go surfing, fishing, snorkeling, hiking, or skiing. In 2015, nearly twenty million people visited Japan. The government expects this number to go even higher as the 2020 Olympics get under way.

Manufacturing

Japan has one of the most valuable manufacturing sectors of any country in the world. The largest Japanese manufacturers are automakers such as Toyota, Nissan, Honda, Subaru, Mazda, and Mitsubishi. Other major manufacturing goods include chemical products and food products. Japan also produces electronic goods such as smartphones, cameras, televisions, stereos, computers, and video game consoles.

Robotics is a rapidly growing industry in Japan. Japan's scientists are world leaders in the field of robotics and artifi-

An engineer works in a robotics lab. Japan has the largest robotics industry in the world.

cial intelligence. Robotics manufacturers build robots to do repetitive work in a variety of fields such as automaking, food processing, and health care. Japanese artificial intelligence experts are developing robots that can learn by themselves to do new tasks. They are also developing humanoid robots, such as one named Aiko Chihira who greets shoppers in a Tokyo department store. She is programmed to speak several languages, including Japanese, English, Chinese, and Japanese Sign Language.

Energy

Japan is one of the most energy-efficient countries in the world. It imports about 85 percent of its fuel in the form of oil, natural gas, and coal. The rest comes from hydroelectric power and nuclear power. Nearly all the rivers in Japan have dams

Commuters fill a train station in Tokyo. Each day, nine million people use the subway in Tokyo and another thirty-one million ride other train systems in the city.

to produce electricity. But nuclear power is the government's choice for controlling costs and providing a constant energy supply. However, after the 2011 earthquake and tsunami that damaged the Fukushima nuclear power plant, all nuclear reactors around the country were ordered to be shut down. Some have been upgraded and are operating again.

Transportation

Public transportation is very efficient in Japan. Trains, buses, boats, and airplanes run on strict schedules. Fuel is expensive, and car drivers are careful to conserve. More than 70 percent of travel is by train. The main islands of Japan are covered in a network of high-speed rail. The passenger trains, called bullet trains, or *shinkansen*, can run at speeds up to 200 miles per hour (320 kph). In March 2016, the shinkansen connecting Honshu with Hokkaido was finished. The tracks run through the longest undersea tunnel in the world. The Seikan Tunnel is a total of 34 miles (54 km) long, of which 14 miles (23 km) lie underwater.

A shinkansen train speeds past Mount Fuji. The bullet trains, which are extremely quiet, connect Tokyo with most major cities in Japan.

CHAPTER 7

National Pride

ANCESTORS OF TODAY'S JAPANESE PEOPLE migrated over the course of thirty thousand years. Three separate cultural groups migrated. The earliest group, the Jomon, arrived between 10,000 BCE and 300 BCE from Siberia and China. They were hunters, gatherers, farmers, and potters. From 300 BCE to 300 CE, the Yayoi culture arrived and settled on Honshu Island. They were weavers, toolmakers, and rice farmers. The various people who lived in Japan mingled to form the Yamato clan in about 300 CE. The Yamato clan took over much of Japan and established the hereditary line of emperors and empresses that survives to this day.

Ethnic Groups

About 98.5 percent of Japanese people trace their heritage to the Yamato clan. Other ethnic groups in Japan today include

Opposite: **Japan has the highest average life expectancy in the world. Japanese people typically live 83.7 years.**

Population of Major Cities (2017 est.):

Tokyo	9,390,048
Yokohama	3,730,158
Osaka	2,702,455
Nagoya	2,306,901
Sapporo	1,958,157

Crowds gather to enjoy a lion dance during a Chinese New Year celebration in Yokohama.

ethnic Koreans, at 0.5 percent, and ethnic Chinese, at 0.4 percent. Other small ethnic groups combine to make 0.6 percent of the population.

When Korean and Chinese workers came to Japan before World War II, some remained and formed close-knit communities. Yokohama is home to Japan's largest Chinatown. On Okinawa, there are U.S. military bases that have operated since the 1940s. Many American servicemen and servicewomen have married Japanese citizens. As a result, there are many people of mixed heritage living on the Okinawa Islands.

One of the oldest of the smaller ethnic groups is the Ainu people of northern Hokkaido. The Ainu people have a different look than the majority of Japanese. They are smaller and have lighter skin and wavy hair. Most men wear thick beards. It is not clear where they migrated from, but many believe it was the northern Ural Mountains, in western Russia. In the remote areas where the Ainu live, there are few opportunities for good jobs and education. Many Ainu are not part of the larger Japanese culture and are often discriminated against. In 2008, the government formally recognized the Ainu as native people of Japan. Efforts are being made to help the Ainu improve their way of living.

The Ryukyuan people are native to the Ryukyu Islands, which include Okinawa. The Ryukyu Islands were an independent nation until Japan conquered them in the seventeenth century. Okinawans are the largest Ryukyuan minority group, with more than one million people.

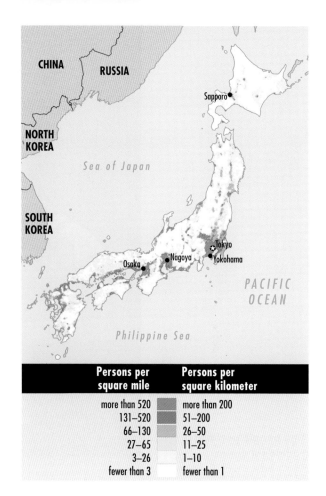

Persons per square mile	Persons per square kilometer
more than 520	more than 200
131–520	51–200
66–130	26–50
27–65	11–25
3–26	1–10
fewer than 3	fewer than 1

Ethnic Japan

Japanese	98.5%
Korean	0.5%
Chinese	0.4%
Other (including Ainu and Okinawan)	0.6%

Language

Nearly everyone in Japan understands standard Japanese. There are dialects—different versions of the language with different accents, vocabulary, and grammar—that vary from region to region, but people are mostly able to understand one another. However, a few languages besides Japanese are spoken in some areas, although they are sometimes also considered dialects of Japanese.

Ainu people perform a traditional dance.

Hachijo is a language spoken on a few small islands south of Tokyo. It is an ancient Japanese language that has never been influenced by modern Japanese, much like the difference between the English of the Middle Ages and the English spoken today. The Ainu people speak a language spoken nowhere else in the world. Very few Ainu language speakers remain. Efforts are being made to preserve the Ainu language by teaching it in schools and printing books written in it.

Several Ryukyuan languages are spoken by people living in the southern island groups. Because people on these remote islands do not interact, many do not understand each other's language or dialect.

The Written Word

Written Japanese typically uses a combination of three sets of symbols: kanji, hiragana, and katakana. Kanji first came to Japan from China in about the fourth century. Kanji are symbols called characters, which represent meanings and sounds. They are used to write such things as nouns, adjectives, adverbs, and verbs. Hiragana and katakana are scripts used to write the sounds of syllables. Another script, called

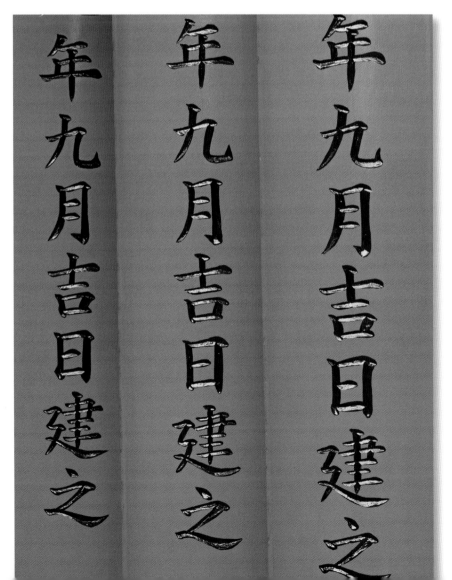

To be able to read Japanese well, people need to know about two thousand characters and symbols.

A Few Japanese Words

Romaji	Hiragana	English
Hai	はい	Yes
Iie	いいえ	No
O-negai shimasu	おねがいします	Please
Arigato	ありがとう	Thank you
Do itashimashite	どういたしまして	You're welcome
Ohayo gozaimasu	おはようございます	Good morning
O-yasumi nasai	おやすみなさい	Good night
Sumimasen	すみません	I am sorry

romaji, is a Latin alphabet that is used to write some foreign and technical words.

Japanese surnames, or family, names, are written in kanji. Many surnames use characters describing things in nature. For instance, the surname Ishikawa, means stone + river. The Japanese place their surname before their given name.

Most middle and high school students wear uniforms to school. It is much less common among elementary school students.

Students in Tokyo work on a project designing cars.

Education

Children attend school for at least nine years. They are required to attend six years of elementary school and three years of junior high school. More than 95 percent of students in rural Japan, and nearly 100 percent living in cities, spend another three years in senior high school. More than half of high school graduates attend a university or junior college. Students attend classes six hours a day, five days a week, and have six weeks of summer vacation and one or two weeks each for winter and spring break. Japan has one of the highest literacy rates in the world; nearly 100 percent of the population can read and write.

Students in Tokyo work on a project designing cars.

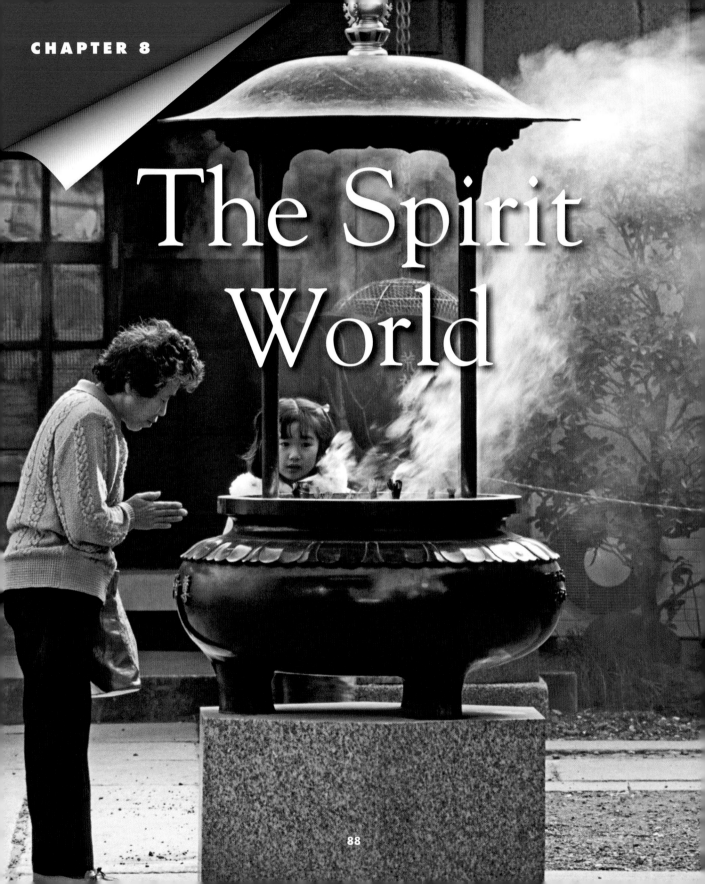

CHAPTER 8

The Spirit World

THE JAPANESE PEOPLE PRACTICE MANY RELIGIONS, often more than one at the same time. Japanese religions are a set of beliefs that help people live a moral life. The shared beliefs unite families and strengthen communities. In Japan, Shinto and Christianity are the religions people tend to turn to for joyous occasions, such as weddings or holidays. People turn to Buddhism when they need comfort from sorrow. In difficult times, people visit Buddhist temples to ask priests to pray for them.

Opposite: **A woman prays at a temple in Tokyo. Most Japanese people do not have a strong adherence to one single religion.**

Shinto

Shinto is Japan's native religion and its oldest. The religion first arrived with the Yayoi people around 300 BCE. The Yayoi

A fox statue stands at an Inari shrine. Inari is the kami of foxes, agriculture, industry, and success.

belonged to clans, and the chief was their spiritual leader. Each clan adopted a god, called a *kami*. A kami represents the spirit inside an object of nature, such as a cedar tree, or a quality in life, such as happiness.

When one clan conquered another, the victorious clan would adopt the defeated clan's kami. Eventually, Shinto became a religion with many gods. The sun goddess, Amaterasu, is Shinto's most important kami, and is considered the founder of Japan. Some families honor their ancestors as kami.

In Shinto, there is no sense of absolute right and wrong, because no one is perfect. People believe that humans are basically good. Any evil in the world is caused by evil spirits. Shinto rituals are often about keeping evil spirits away. People visit places of worship to purify themselves, pray, and make offerings to the kami to protect them from suffering and evil.

Buddhism

Buddhism was introduced to Japan by Chinese and Korean migrants in the 500s CE. By the seventh century, Buddhism had become the religion of the nobility. Buddhism then spread rapidly.

The Buddhist religion began with an Indian prince who became known as the Buddha, meaning the "Enlightened One." He taught people to be kind and thoughtful, even as

The reclining Buddha statue at Nanzoin Temple on Kyushu, in southern Japan, is 134 feet (41 m) long. It is one of the largest bronze statues in the world.

Confucius

Confucius was a sixth century Chinese philosopher. His teachings greatly impressed the Japanese imperial court. Confucius taught honor, loyalty, obedience, and kindness. He was known for making simple statements that expressed important ideas, such as "Our greatest glory is not in never falling, but in getting up every time we do"; or "Respect yourself and others will respect you." The Tokugawa shoguns later adopted Confucian philosophy and incorporated it into their rule. Confucian philosophy continues to influence Japanese culture today.

they lived a life of suffering. In Japan, people became devoted to their Buddhist rulers. In the eighth century, the imperial government named Buddhism the national religion.

Christianity

In 1542, Europeans first came to Japan. Some were Portuguese merchants, but others were Christian missionaries. The missionaries converted many Japanese to their religion, including nobles.

Japan's leaders sometimes felt threatened by Christianity. When the Tokugawa shoguns came to power, they accused Christians of not showing respect for Shinto, Buddhism, or other Japanese traditions. In the 1630s, many Christians took part in a failed rebellion against the shogunate. After defeating the rebels, the shogunate executed many Christian fighters and banned Christianity as a religion. Japanese Christians were forced to practice their religion in secret.

Religious Changes

The early years of the Meiji period brought religious change. After taking command of the military, Emperor Meiji discouraged Confucianism because it was associated with the shogunate. He also wanted to reduce the authority of the Buddhist priests so he took away much of their land. The emperor believed Shinto, the oldest Japanese religion, would help support his new government. He named Shinto the state religion.

Religious freedom came about after the Meiji period. Buddhism came back into favor, although Shinto remained the religion of the imperial family and most of the people. Christians were once again able to practice their faith openly.

Japanese Catholics take part in a service. The nation is home to about 440,000 Catholics.

Places of Worship

Shinto believers pray at small altars in their homes and gardens or by visiting a shrine. Shinto shrines honor the kami. People come to pay respect, as well as to pray for good luck or seek protection from evil spirits. People also visit to celebrate holidays and special events such as weddings, the birth of a child, or New Year's.

Shrines contain special features. At the entrance to a shrine stands one or more tall gates, or torii. The torii is often made of wood with long beams across the top. Guarding each side of the entrance is a statue that depicts an imaginary animal that com-

Japanese people rinse their hands to purify themselves before entering a Shinto shrine.

bines a dog and a lion. Shrines that are devoted to Inari, the kami of rice, are guarded by statues of foxes. Near the entrance is a trough or fountain of water that people use to purify, or clean, their hands. Inside the shrine are two halls. The main hall is where the most sacred objects of the shrine are hidden in special chambers. The other hall is the offering hall, where people pray and leave coins as offerings. Some shrines have stages where dances and ceremonies are held.

There are more than one hundred thousand Shinto shrines in Japan. The largest and most sacred shrine is Ise Jingu, which is dedicated to the sun goddess, Amaterasu. Ise Jingu is a massive group of buildings, gardens, and smaller shrines. Over the course of the year, many rituals are performed to pray for the imperial family, world peace, and bountiful harvests.

Making a Wish

Most visitors enter the offering hall of a Shinto shrine to make a wish or seek good fortune. Many shrines sell small wooden "wishing plaques," called *ema*. Ema are

painted with fanciful images such as animals, scenery, sailing ships, historical figures, or toys. People write their names and their wishes on the ema and hang them at the shrine. During the school year, shrines that are known for the god of study are filled with ema hung by students hoping for luck in passing their exams.

Shinto shrines throughout Japan sell strips of paper fortunes called *omikuji*. For the price of a coin or two, people select their omikuji from a box. The strips of paper are rolled up tightly, and inside are poems that either promise good fortune or warn of bad fortune. Traditionally, people tie their omikuji onto trees growing around the shrine, so that good fortune will come true and bad fortune will go away.

The original Golden Pavilion was completed in 1397. It burned down in 1950 but was then reconstructed.

Religion in Japan

Shinto	83.9%
Buddhism	71.4%
Christianity	2%
Other	7.8%

(Confucianism, Islam, Hinduism, Sikhism)

Note: Many people belong to multiple religions

Buddhist houses of worship are called temples. There are more than seventy-five thousand Buddhist temples in cities, villages, and mountain settings. Temples are often surrounded by trees, gardens, or wilderness. Other features include an entrance gate, a main hall, and sometimes a three- or five-story tower called a pagoda. The main hall houses sacred objects such as statues, scrolls, and a bell. People visit temples to meditate, honor their ancestors, and participate in festivals and rituals. The Golden Pavilion in Kyoto is the most famous temple. It is covered in gold leaf.

Christian churches and Confucian temples are also found throughout Japan. Many of the Christian churches are Roman Catholic. The oldest was built in Nagasaki in 1864. Confucian temples are often connected to schools teaching Confucian philosophy. There are also Hindu and Sikh temples and Muslim mosques.

Religious Festivals

Every shrine and temple in Japan holds a religious festival. Shinto festivals are called *matsuri*. The main event of a matsuri, which means "sacred procession," is a parade. People dress in special clothes and carry a portable shrine holding the spirit of their community's kami. The parade travels from house to house or street to street. In this way, the kami blesses its community. People make offerings to the local shrine and later feast, dance, and play games.

People carry a shrine through the streets of Tokyo during a matsuri.

CHAPTER 9

Grace and Beauty

THE JAPANESE PEOPLE ENJOY A RICH CULTURAL LIFE. From early history until today, artists, writers, poets, musicians, and others have produced a culture uniquely Japanese. Their creativity has inspired people worldwide.

Literature

Japanese literature began with storytelling. The first Japanese books date back as far as the eighth century. Some of the first included a history of Japan, a book of Japanese legends and myths, and a book of Japanese history, folklore, and geography titled *Records of Wind and Earth*. One of the world's first novels was written by a lady-in-waiting named Murasaki Shikibu in the eleventh century. It was titled *The Tale of Genji* and told stories of romance and intrigue in the imperial court.

Basho: Haiku Master

Haiku is a special form of Japanese poetry. A haiku poet uses just a few words to create a mental picture, usually of nature. A haiku is most often written in three lines. The first and last lines have five syllables and the second line has seven. When the haiku are translated into English, the number of syllables sometimes varies.

Matsuo Basho was born in 1644 and became Japan's most famous haiku poet. The son of a samurai, he spent a few years studying literature and Buddhist meditation. Later, he traveled around Japan and wrote haiku describing what he saw. Here is one of his haiku:

The clouds come and go,
providing a rest for all
the moon viewers

For centuries, Japanese authors wrote about their close bond with nature. Many also wrote about the bravery of samurai warriors. After the horrors of World War II, Japanese writers turned to a wider variety of subjects, from solemn novels to science fiction. The first Japanese writer to win the Nobel Prize in Literature, the world's most prestigious literary prize, was Yasunari Kawabata, who wrote sorrowful, lyrical novels. In 1994, Kenzaburo Oe won the same prize. His works describe imaginary worlds and problems in society. Other well-known writers are Banana Yoshimoto, whose work includes the popular novel, *Lizard*, and Haruki Murakami, who has won many awards. His books have been printed in more than fifty languages.

Music and Dance

Many Japanese dances are ancient and are based on Shinto and Buddhist rituals. Traditional Shinto dances focus on wishing for something, such as a good harvest, or celebrating a joyous event, such as the arrival of spring. Some dancers wear hand-painted, hand-carved wooden masks and colorful,

elaborate costumes. The dancers are accompanied by drums and the *fue*, a flute-like instrument.

Dances based on Buddhist beliefs are often about hardship and loss. Bon Odori is one such dance. Bon Odori dancers welcome spirits of the dead during the Obon festival. Each region has its own style of bon dances. Most bon dancers perform around a tall wooden structure called a *yagura*. The dancers' movements express the lifestyle of their region. For example, dancers in a mining town may mimic digging, pushing a heavy cart, and lighting lanterns in underground tunnels. Dancers in fishing villages may imitate dragging a net, steering a boat, and hauling in fish.

Yosakoi is a dance form that blends traditional Japanese dance movements with modern movement. The style is very lively and upbeat. Most yosakoi dances are performed by large teams.

Taiko drumming is a Japanese style of percussion. The word *taiko* means "fat drum." Taiko drums are often very large. While performing, drummers of big taiko stand in a crouched position with their legs spread wide. They wave their arms in dramatic movements and beat the drums with great force. Taiko drumming is very loud and very fast. Originally, taiko drummers performed on battlefields to scare the enemy. They also beat the drums to send orders to distant troops.

Another classic Japanese instrument is the *koto*, a stringed instrument similar to a zither. Koto music is popular during the New Year's holidays.

Theater

Noh is one of the oldest forms of theater in the world. It became popular with the nobility during the Tokugawa shogunate. Noh actors are backed by singers and musicians who play flutes and drums. Actors do not have many spoken lines. Instead, their movements tell most of the story. There are five types of traditional Noh plays: *kami* plays are stories about gods at Shinto shrines; *shura mono* are battle plays; *katsura mono* are plays about women performed by men; *kirinoh mono* are plays about devils, demons, beasts, and supernatural creatures; and *zatsunoh* are Noh plays that fall into none of the other categories. Present-day Noh plays are called *gendaimono*.

Kabuki theater was created in the seventeenth century by a female dancer who was an attendant at a Shinto shrine. Unlike Noh theater, kabuki entertained the working people rather than the nobility. Gradually, kabuki came to be performed

only by men. Actors mime and sing and dance in exaggerated ways. There are dramatic battle scenes and acrobatic displays. Costumes and makeup are extravagant.

Taiko drummers use thick sticks to pound out their rhythm.

Manga and Anime

Manga is a uniquely Japanese type of illustrated book. Characters in the books are generally drawn in black and white and have cartoon-like facial features and bodies. Manga books are not just comic books. There are many kinds of manga books, such as action, mystery, science fiction, romance, and sports. Manga books are written and illustrated for people of all ages.

Anime is a type of Japanese animated filmmaking. Anime movies are often based on manga characters. Some famous

Master Filmmaker

Akira Kurosawa was an award-winning filmmaker and one of the most influential film directors in the world. He directed more than thirty films and was the first to bring Japanese filmmaking to the Western world. His films were bold and had great attention to detail. His first film to be recognized internationally was *Rashomon*, a tale of thieves in feudal Japan. His other films include *Seven Samurai*, *Dersu Uzala*, about a Siberian hermit, and *Tora! Tora! Tora!,* about the Japanese bombing of Pearl Harbor. Kurosawa won two Academy Awards and many other international film prizes.

anime series are *Dragon Ball Z*, *Sailor Moon*, *One Piece*, and *Pokémon*. Many people consider Hayao Miyazaki to be the greatest anime filmmaker of all time. His movies, including *Spirited Away* and *Howl's Moving Castle*, have been seen all over the world. Anime and manga characters are a part of many Japanese home video games. Nintendo, Sony, and Sega introduced some of the first video games in the early 1980s. The games, such as *Dragon Quest*, *Super Mario*, *Pokémon*, and *The Legend of Zelda*, are popular around the world.

Crafts

Japan is renowned for its exquisite crafts. Pottery, first crafted for everyday use, became more decorative and detailed over time. In the era of the Tokugawa shogunate, the ritual of the Japanese tea ceremony grew widespread. Beautiful ceramic tea sets were highly prized. Exports of Japanese pottery increased. Of special interest to foreign buyers was Japan's

In a scene from Hayao Miyazaki's *Howl's Moving Castle*, a young woman discovers that a spell has turned her old. Miyazaki's films are renowned for their artistry, devotion to nature, and complex female characters.

fine porcelain ware. The most desirable had a pale blue-green (celadon) glaze. Japanese pottery is considered among the finest in the world.

The first Japanese weavers made simple cloth from grasses and rope. By around 200 CE, Japanese weavers and dyers began creating beautiful textiles in silk. As trade with foreign merchants grew, Japan also acquired cotton and brocade, a heavy embroidered fabric. The nobility wore brocade as well as delicately dyed and hand-painted silk kimonos. Kimonos are tied with a wide sash called an obi.

In the seventeenth century, the Tokugawa shogunate imposed strict rules on what clothing each social class could wear. Only the nobility could wear silk and brocade. A farmer could raise silkworms and a weaver could weave silk into cloth, but neither could wear silk. The rules enraged the merchant class, who set to producing a variety of patterns, weaves, and dyes out of other fabrics. The designs rivaled in beauty the clothing of the noble class. Two famous types of Japanese textiles from this era are called *kasuri* and *shibori*. Kasuri is a difficult process in which threads are dyed before they are woven. It takes great skill to lay out the pattern on the loom. Shibori is a dye process like modern tie-dye, but very precise. Kyoto was, and remains today, a center for Japanese textile production. After centuries of producing beautiful textiles, Japan today has developed an important fashion industry.

Art and Sculpture

Some of the world's oldest and finest sculptures can be found in Japan. Nearly all ancient sculptures are Buddhist. Most are likenesses of the Buddha. Others are elaborately carved gods and animals that "guard" temple gates. The sculptures are made of bronze, stone, or wood. One sculptor, a Buddhist monk named Enku, traveled all over Japan carving many thousands of wooden Buddhas. Thousands still exist. To this day, sculpture is an important and prominent form of art in Japan. Most public and many private spaces contain sculptures. Although modern sculpture is not generally Buddhist, modern sculptors are inspired by Buddhist beliefs, such as simplicity and peacefulness.

The first form of Japanese painting used black ink. Artists painted landscapes and portraits with precise and simple brush-

strokes. From the twelfth to fourteenth centuries, artists painted on paper scrolls. The scrolls portrayed history, legends, and life in the imperial court. In the seventeenth century, Japanese

An elegant sculpture of a mask sits along Lake Toyako in Hokkaido.

Origami

Origami is the art of folding paper into shapes. Most Japanese schoolchildren first learn the craft in kindergarten. Origami as an art came to Japan from China in the seventh century. Enthusiasm for origami grew during the Tokugawa shogunate. Today, the most famous origami figure is the crane, a bird sacred to the Japanese.

One legend says whoever folds a thousand cranes will be granted a wish.

After World War II, the practice of folding cranes took on greater meaning. A girl named Sadako was two years old when the atomic bomb was dropped on Hiroshima. When she was eleven, she grew very ill. Sadako decided to fold a thousand cranes in the hope that her wish to recover would come true. She died after folding 644 cranes. Her classmates folded the rest in the hope that their wish for world peace would come true. Since that time, children all over the world have been making origami cranes, symbolizing their hope for world peace.

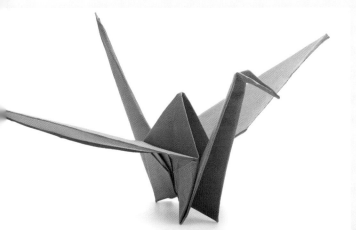

Katsushika Hokusai created *The Great Wave* in about 1830.

artists developed printmaking. They carved images onto a block of wood. Then they spread ink onto the woodblock and pressed the woodblock onto paper. In this way, they could create many copies of one image. One of the most famous woodblock prints is *The Great Wave*. In this print, the artist, Katsushika Hokusai, shows a huge wave about to crash onto small fishing boats below. A tiny Mount Fuji is in the distance. Japanese woodblock printing remains an important art form.

Architecture

Most early Japanese buildings were made of wood. Many houses had thatched roofs. Shrines and larger houses had steep wooden roofs to shed rain and snow. By the eighth century, Japanese

architecture was influenced by China and Korea. Temples and palaces had wide courtyards, gardens, and pagoda roofs. Some pagoda roofs in Japan contained five tiers, each level smaller than the one below. The tiers represented the ancient five elements: earth, water, fire, wind, and sky. Pagoda roofs had few nails holding them together. Instead, each piece of wood was carved with slots and fitted together. Because the buildings were not rigid, they could withstand earthquakes.

Modern architecture in Japan has many styles. Tokyo and other large cities have tall, gleaming skyscrapers. The largest building in Japan, and one of the tallest in the world, is the SkyTree. The SkyTree has shops and an aquarium at its base and two observation decks at the top. The center of the SkyTree has a column, which is like the column in the center of a pagoda. Just as in a pagoda, the center column helps the SkyTree withstand earthquakes.

A brightly lit pagoda rises above cherry trees in Kyoto.

CHAPTER 10

Work and Play

THE JAPANESE LIFESTYLE CHANGED DRAMATICALLY in the middle of the twentieth century. Before World War II, many people made their living on farms or as loggers, miners, or craftspeople. They lived and worked in rural areas. But that changed during and after the war, when people moved to cities to work in factories. After the war, Japan modernized quickly, as more people left the countryside for careers in offices.

Opposite: **Girls take part in a festival in southern Japan.**

Housing

Traditionally, a Japanese family living in one house consisted of children, parents, and grandparents. But today, city-dwelling families are mostly parents and children who live separately from grandparents. Many families live in suburbs miles outside of downtown, and people commute by train to work, often one to two hours each way. Closer to downtown, families live in apartments.

Traditional Japanese houses are made of wood, and although today some newer houses are made of steel and concrete, inside they have a traditional feel. Most floors are wooden, but some are covered in tatami, mats of woven grass. Tatami is cool in summer and warm in winter. Most homes have special tatami rooms, which are used as guest rooms. A tatami room has few pieces of furniture. Many have a small alcove that features art or a flower arrangement. Walls and doors are made of wooden frames with canvas or rice paper set into the frames. Some people sit directly on the tatami, and others sit on cushions. When a tatami room is used for

Many Japanese inns feature simple, peaceful tatami rooms.

Good Manners

The Japanese people believe that the best way to get along is to be cooperative, polite, and respectful. Good manners are very important. Children learn at a young age to speak with respect to others. Students call students in higher grades *senpai*, meaning senior, and their teachers *sensei*, meaning master. Children and adults use *san* or sometimes *sama* after a person's last name to show respect. *San* is similar to Mr. or Mrs., and *sama* is used for situations requiring more formality. Relatives and close friends often add *chan* to a girl's name and *kun* to a boy's name. It is like adding *ie* to a name, such as Susie or Freddie.

Being humble is good manners in Japan. Japanese people do not like to hear bragging, and in fact, they will go to great lengths to make themselves seem unworthy. For example, gift-giving is very common. People enjoy making a show of presenting a gift, yet they will often begin apologizing right away, saying that the gift is not very good.

Bowing is another way the Japanese people show respect for each other. Some bows are deep and others

are slight, sometimes just a nod of the head. People bow when they are introduced, or when greeting someone or making an apology. Shopkeepers bow to their customers. Visitors to shrines bow to the gods. Athletes bow to their opponents before a game or event. Men bow with their hands to their sides and women bring their hands together and rest them on their legs when bowing.

sleeping, a folding mattress called a futon is laid on the floor.

Manners and good hygiene are expected in a Japanese home. Everyone removes their shoes before entering. Slippers are often placed by the door. Special slippers are also placed inside the bathroom, where the toilet is, to use only there. Guests as well as family members wear them while in the bathroom. Japanese homes have a separate bathing room that includes a soaking tub. People wash and rinse first, and then enter the bath to soak and relax.

Western foods are increasingly popular in Japan. In a recent survey, Japanese children voted pizza their favorite food. Hamburgers came in third.

Clothing

For centuries, Japanese men, women, and children have worn kimonos. A kimono is a formal robe, traditionally made of silk or brocade, tied with a wide sash called an obi. Kimonos are still worn for special occasions, such as weddings, graduations, and some holidays. They are tight and difficult to wear and move in. Women's kimonos are expensive and often very detailed. Men generally wear black kimonos. People also wear casual ones made of wool or raw silk. Although it is still common to see people wearing kimonos, few people do so in everyday life. In summer, however, young people wear a kimono-like garment called a *yukata* for parties and festivals. A yukata is a lightweight cotton robe with bright, bold patterns. It is inexpensive and more comfortable to wear than a kimono.

Today, most people, especially in cities, wear Western-style clothing. Young people wear jeans, women wear dresses and business suits, and men with office jobs wear suits. Japanese people tend to be very stylish. Japanese fashion designers often blend traditional looks and fabrics with sleek, modern designs. Many young people in Japan have a distinct fashion sense. They blend colors, patterns, styles, and old and new into unique and individual looks. One popular style is called *kawaii*, which means "cute." Kawaii is seen everywhere in shirts, shoes, high fashion, and hairstyles, as well as store displays, toys, and household objects. Hello Kitty, for example, is kawaii, as are many manga and anime characters.

Food

Japanese farmers and fishers provide their country with a wide variety of traditional foods. Western-style food is also becoming more of a regular part of the national diet. Food, even in the simplest meals, is often artfully served.

A typical Japanese meal is plain rice served with fish or meat and vegetables, as well as soup, usually *miso* (fermented soybeans), and pickled vegetables. Favorite dishes include *tempura*, made with vegetables, fish, or prawns that are dipped in egg and flour batter and deep-fried. *Sushi* is a small ball of sticky rice mixed with vinegar, sugar, and salt and topped with seafood or eggs. Rice can be rolled with vegetables, egg, or seafood, and then wrapped in a thin piece of seaweed, called *nori*, to create *maki sushi*. Sushi is served with a horseradish called *wasabi*, pickled ginger root, and soy sauce. *Sashimi* is thin slices of raw fish eaten with soy sauce and wasabi.

A favorite dish for special occasions is *sukiyaki*, which is cooked at the table. Ingredients include slices of beef, vegetables such as chrysanthemum leaves, and thin noodles. *Shabu-shabu* is another popular special dish. It is cooked in a pot of hot broth at the table. People use chopsticks to pick up thin slices of beef and vegetables and dip them into the broth to cook.

Soba and *udon* noodles are two of the more popular types of noodles. When people eat noodles, they slurp loudly. It is not rude, but rather the quickest way to cool the noodles so that they can be eaten while they are still hot and flavorful.

Sushi and maki sushi are made fresh at a fish market in Tokyo.

The Way of Tea

Tea has long been the most popular beverage in Japan, although young people now drink more coffee. Tea came from China in the sixth century. It was a luxury, and special teahouses and gardens were built. Teahouses are simple buildings with few furnishings. The point of the tea ceremony is to get away from daily living and enjoy calm and peace.

The ceremony begins with a host who prepares tea and sweet cakes. Sweet cakes are decorative and attractively arranged. When guests arrive, they stop at a water basin to wash their hands and mouth. When they enter, they bow to the host. Once seated, the host first serves the sweet cakes. Then the host makes the tea in a cup. Before drinking the tea, the guest turns the cup three times to avoid drinking from the front of the cup, drinks it in a few sips, and then wipes the rim to clean it. The bitterness of the tea combined with the sweetness of the cakes creates a feeling of balance and peace. The tea ceremony is no longer common today.

Sweets

These days, Western-style cakes, cookies, and candies are extremely popular in Japan, but people also enjoy Japanese desserts. Several favorite desserts today are made with *mochi*, a dough made from sticky rice. Mochi is often rolled into balls and stuffed with anko (a sweet bean paste) or served in chunks in a sweet bean soup. *Sakuramochi* is a mochi wrapped in a pickled cherry leaf. *Dorayaki* is a pancake sandwich traditionally stuffed with anko and sometimes chestnuts. A special dessert called *hanabiramochi* is usually made for New Year's. It is pink

Work and Play   **117**

Dango, a dessert made from rice flour, is often eaten in the spring, during celebrations when flowers are in bloom.

mochi and white anko mixed with miso. The pink and white represents an *ume* (plum) blossom, a symbol for a new start.

Sports

Sports are an important part of life in Japan. After studying or working hard, people enjoy playing sports and cheering on their favorite athletes and teams. Schoolchildren join school soccer, baseball, and basketball teams, and many people continue playing team sports through high school and beyond. Many Japanese also enjoy sports like golf or tennis, and they like to hike, swim, ski, skate, and surf.

Sumo wrestling has a long history, and the sport is accompanied by many elaborate rituals.

Probably the most popular traditional Japanese sport is sumo wrestling, which is more than 1,500 years old. It began as a Shinto ritual where it was believed sumo wrestlers fought with the gods. Remnants of the ritual still appear, such as spreading salt around the ring to purify it. Some sumo wrestlers weigh more than 300 pounds (130 kg). They dress in tiny loincloths and wear their hair in the ancient samurai style of a topknot. During a match, the wrestlers push, pull, and slap each other. The winner is the one who smashes the other to the ground or throws him out of the ring.

The most internationally known traditional Japanese sports are martial arts. There are four main Japanese forms: kendo, karate, aikido, and judo. Kendo is Japan's oldest martial art. It is similar to fencing. Kendo practitioners once jousted with swords, but today they use bamboo blades. The word *karate* means "empty hand." The meaning of the empty hand in karate is that one never strikes first. Karate is made up of kicks, blows, and blocks using arms, fists, feet, and legs. Aikido is a newer martial art. It was developed by a former soldier and spiritual leader named Morihei Ueshiba. It is not an aggressive martial art; rather it is based on defensive, dance-like movements. *Judo* means "gentle way." Judo turns the speed and power of the opponent back against him or her. To some it is self-defense, to others it is a friendly sport, and to still others it is physical fitness.

Japanese archery, called *kyudo*, is another ancient Shinto sport. Before sword fighting, archery was a samurai warrior's most important skill. Kyudo archers aim and shoot in slow, graceful movements. The target is small, and hitting the target is often less important than the archer's form.

The Japanese enjoy modern sports, too. Fans are wild about their national soccer team, Samurai Blue. Baseball is also popular. Japan has twelve professional baseball teams and one national team, named Samurai Japan. The World Baseball Classic is held every three years, and Samurai Japan won in 2006 and 2009, and is always ranked in the top five teams. Some top Japanese baseball players, such as Ichiro Suzuki, have played in the American major leagues. Suzuki spent most of his career with the Orix Blue Wave in Japan and the Seattle Mariners in the United States. He is one of the most popular stars in Japan.

Japan has participated in the Summer Olympics since

1912. Japanese teams have won medals in events such as swimming, tennis, wrestling, canoeing, gymnastics, and volleyball. Tokyo hosted the Summer Olympics in 1964 and will again in 2020.

Japan has also hosted the Winter Olympics twice, once in Sapporo and once in Nagano. In the 2014 Olympics, a high-flying teenager named Yuzuru Hanyu won Japan's first gold medal in men's figure skating. His teammate, forty-one-year-old Noriaki Kasai, became the oldest ski jumping medalist in Olympic history.

An aikido expert throws her opponent during a demonstration of the sport.

A bride and groom walk to the Shinto shrine where they will be married.

Birth, Marriage, and Death Customs

Japanese families rejoice at the birth of a child. Seven days after a child is born, the family holds a small naming ceremony. Tradition holds that newborn children are godly. They are dressed in white to symbolize their purity. When the children are about a month old, they are brought to a Shinto shrine. Parents want their children to feel the spirits of their community. Friends and relatives also join the families, often bringing gifts.

Some Japanese wedding ceremonies are held at a Shinto

shrine, and some Japanese people marry at a Christian church. At a traditional wedding, the bride wears an elaborate white kimono with an enormous headpiece. The groom wears a black kimono. The Shinto priest says prayers over the couple before they perform a ritual known as *san-san-kudo*. The term means three-three-nine times. Nine is considered a lucky number. The bride takes three sips of a drink called sake from one cup, the groom takes three sips from a second cup, and then the bride takes three more sips from a third cup. Since it is an ancient ritual, the exact meaning is not certain. Most believe it represents love, wisdom, and happiness.

Only a few guests attend the wedding ceremony. Family and friends are invited to the reception. A meal of traditional Japanese food is served, although Western meals are becoming more popular. Sometimes there are entertainers, dances, or party games. The bride and groom give gifts to their guests, and the guests give the couple money in decorative envelopes.

In difficult times, Japanese people tend to turn to Buddhism. Nearly 85 percent of Japanese funerals are Buddhist ceremonies. A Buddhist funeral is a farewell ceremony. People are comforted that their departed loved ones have become spirits traveling to a pure and peaceful land. Most families have a small family shrine. When a family member dies, the shrine is covered in white paper. A few items such as flowers and candles are placed on a small altar. A knife is sometimes placed nearby, to help the departing spirit defend against evil spirits. Friends and relatives first attend a wake. They bring gifts of money in black and white envelopes. When they leave, the guests are given small gifts. During the funeral, the Buddhist priest prays and gives the deceased a new name, to help the spirit move away from the world. Families often hold memorial services on the seventh, forty-ninth, and one hundredth day after a loved one dies, as well as three, seven, thirteen, and thirty-three years afterward.

Holidays and Festivals

Japan celebrates more than a dozen national holidays and thousands of festivals, called *matsuri*. Every city, town, and village holds at least one matsuri. Most matsuri are based on Shinto rit-

National Holidays

New Year's	January 1
Coming of Age Day	Second Monday of January
National Foundation Day	February 11
Spring Equinox Day	March 20 or March 21
Showa Day	April 29
Constitution Memorial Day	May 3
Greenery Day	May 4
Children's Day	May 5
Marine Day	Third Monday of July
Mountain Day	August 11
Respect for the Aged Day	Third Monday of September
Autumn Equinox Day	September 22 or 23
Sports Day	Second Monday of October
Culture Day	November 3
Labor Thanksgiving Day	November 23

The Emperor's Birthday is also a national holiday.

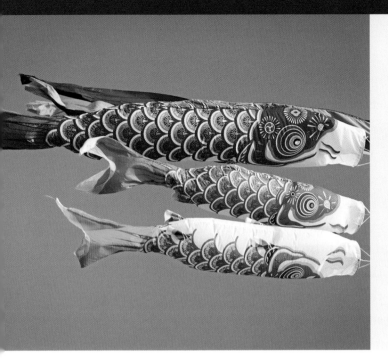

Children's Day

Children's Day, a national holiday celebrated on May 5, was once known as Boy's Day. Girl's Day was held on March 3. The two holidays were combined in 1948 to celebrate the happiness of all children and to honor their mothers. Girl's Day was celebrated by the gift of dolls passed down from mothers to daughters over generations. The special food of Girl's Day was a three-layered mochi treat, colored with flowers. Boy's Day was celebrated with gifts of samurai dolls and flags. On Children's Day today, flags shaped like carps are flown everywhere. Carps are a special symbol of strength and bravery.

uals. Many villages celebrate their matsuri when rice is planted in spring and harvested in autumn. In those festivals, villagers carry a portable shrine around to bless the town and people. They make offerings of rice and fruit to the gods. They dress in traditional matsuri costumes, eat special foods, and play games.

New Year's Eve is celebrated at the end of several weeks' worth of cleaning, paying off debts, and otherwise doing away with the "dirt" of the old year. In late December, Japanese hold "forgetting of the year" parties and decorate their homes with wreaths of good omens. Around midnight, Buddhist temples ring out bell chimes. On New Year's Day, family members gather to share a meal of special holiday foods.

Setsubun is a holiday in February that has its beginnings in the ancient belief that on that day, the real world is closest to the spirit world. Demons and evil spirits could invade the real world and cause strange things to happen. For this festival, families roast soybean treats. Parents don demon masks, and children throw soybeans at them to scare the "demons" away.

Summertime brings many of Japan's biggest and most colorful festivals. The oldest and most famous festival is the Gion Matsuri in Kyoto, which lasts the entire month of July. The festival dates to the ninth century when a plague struck and the people marched through the streets and pleaded with the gods to cure them. The main event is a huge procession of decorated floats that are hauled through the city. Another of Japan's largest festivals is Osaka's Tenjin Matsuri, which honors the god of art and literature. It is also one of the world's largest boating festivals. After parades and musical performances, roughly three thousand people dressed in ancient costumes board a fleet of boats and sail upriver. Another summertime festival is the Kanto Matsuri, or pole lantern festival. The highlight of this festival is when performers balance 40-foot (12 m) poles on their heads, hands, hips, or shoulders. Attached to each pole are dozens of lit paper lanterns.

Snow Sculpture

A somewhat new but popular festival is the Sapporo Snow Festival held in Hokkaido. It began in 1950, when a high school art teacher and his students built snow sculptures in the city park. Today, two million people come at the height of snow season to see spectacular snow sculptures built by teams from around the world. A recent favorite took a month to build. It was a massive Star Wars sculpture, 50 feet (15 m) tall and 72 feet (22 m) wide.

Obon, Japan's largest Buddhist festival, is celebrated for a week in the middle of August. During Obon, people remember the spirits of ancestors, who are said to return home at this time. People go to their hometowns to gather with friends and family. Graves are cleaned and covered with offerings of food and flowers to welcome the spirits. Festivities include music, taiko drumming, dancing, and special foods. On the last day of Obon, people escort the ancestral spirits back to their graves, sending along flowers and other offerings to ward off evil spirits. In some places, people light lanterns and set them afloat to drift out into the sea.

People set lanterns bearing candles afloat during Obon.

Timeline

JAPANESE HISTORY		WORLD HISTORY	
The Jomon culture arises in Japan.	10,000 BCE		
		ca. 2500 BCE	The Egyptians build the pyramids and the Sphinx in Giza.
Jimmu is crowned the first Japanese emperor.	660 BCE	ca. 563 BCE	The Buddha is born in India.
The Yamato clan forms in Japan.	300 CE		
		313 CE	The Roman emperor Constantine legalizes Christianity.
Buddhism arrives in Japan.	500s	610	The Prophet Muhammad begins preaching a new religion called Islam.
The Great Eastern Temple is built.	752	1054	The Eastern (Orthodox) and Western (Roman Catholic) Churches break apart.
		1095	The Crusades begin.
Minamoto Yoritomo establishes the shogunate system.	1100s	1215	King John seals the Magna Carta.
The Mongol army attacks Japan.	1274	1300s	The Renaissance begins in Italy.
		1347	The plague sweeps through Europe.
		1453	Ottoman Turks capture Constantinople, conquering the Byzantine Empire.
The Age of Warring States begins.	1467	1492	Columbus arrives in North America.
		1500s	Reformers break away from the Catholic Church, and Protestantism is born.
The Tokugawa shogunate begins.	1603	1776	The U.S. Declaration of Independence is signed.
		1789	The French Revolution begins.
U.S. Navy vessels sail into Tokyo harbor to try to open Japan to U.S. ships.	1853	1865	The American Civil War ends.
Mutsuhito becomes emperor, beginning the Meiji period.	1867	1879	The first practical lightbulb is invented.
Japan's first constitution is written.	1889		

JAPANESE HISTORY

China and Japan go to war.	**1894**
Japan defeats Russia in a war.	**1905**
Japan attacks Pearl Harbor, Hawaii.	**1941**
The United States drops two atomic bombs on Japan, prompting Japan's surrender in World War II.	**1945**
Japan's current constitution is adopted.	**1947**
An economic boom begins in Japan.	**1950s**
Japan experiences a financial crash.	**Early 1990s**
An earthquake and tsunami kill more than 15,000 people near the Honshu coast.	**2011**
Mount Ontake erupts, killing more than 50 hikers.	**2014**
Yuriko Koike is elected the first woman governor of Tokyo.	**2016**

WORLD HISTORY

1914	World War I begins.
1917	The Bolshevik Revolution brings communism to Russia.
1929	A worldwide economic depression begins.
1939	World War II begins.
1945	World War II ends.
1969	Humans land on the Moon.
1975	The Vietnam War ends.
1989	The Berlin Wall is torn down as communism crumbles in Eastern Europe.
1991	The Soviet Union breaks into separate states.
2001	Terrorists attack the World Trade Center in New York City and the Pentagon near Washington, D.C.
2004	A tsunami in the Indian Ocean destroys coastlines in Africa, India, and Southeast Asia.
2008	The United States elects its first African American president.
2016	Donald Trump is elected U.S. president.

Fast Facts

Official name: Japan

National anthem: "Kimigayo" ("The Emperor's Reign")

Official language: Japanese

Tokyo

National flag

Rainstorm

Official religion:	None
Type of government:	Constitutional monarchy and parliamentary democracy
Head of state:	Emperor
Head of government:	Prime minister
Area of country:	145,914 square miles (377,915 sq km)
Latitude and longitude of Tokyo:	35°41' N 139°41' E
Bordering bodies of water:	Sea of Japan to the west, Sea of Okhotsk to the north, East China Sea to the south, Pacific Ocean to the east
Highest elevation:	Mount Fuji 12,388 feet (3,776 m) above sea level
Lowest elevation:	Lake Hachiro, 13 feet (4 m) below sea level
Longest river:	Shinano, 228 miles (367 km)
Deepest lake:	Lake Tazawa, 1,388 feet (423 m)
Number of islands:	6,852
Number of inhabited islands:	426
Average high temperature:	In Tokyo, 85°F (29°C) in July, 49°F (10°C) in January
Average low temperature:	In Tokyo, 71°F (22°C) in July, 34°F (1°C) in January
Average annual precipitation:	In Tokyo, 55 inches (140 cm)

Golden Pavilion Temple

National population (2017 est.): 126,790,000

Population of major cities (2017 est.):

Tokyo	9,390,048
Yokohama	3,730,158
Osaka	2,702,455
Nagoya	2,306,901
Sapporo	1,958,157

Landmarks:
- ▶ *Mount Fuji,* Shizuoka
- ▶ *Golden Pavilion Temple,* Kyoto
- ▶ *Toshogu Shrine,* Nikko
- ▶ *Ginza,* Tokyo
- ▶ *Shiretoko National Park,* Hokkaido

Economy: Japan's greatest source of income comes from manufacturing, including electronics and passenger cars and trucks. Fishing is a successful industry. Tourism and other service industries are important to the economy. Major agricultural products include rice, vegetables, and fruits such as apples and mandarin oranges.

Currency: The Yen. In 2017, US$1 equaled 112 yen.

System of weights and measures: Metric system

Literacy rate: 99%

Currency

Schoolchildren

Akira Kurosawa

Common Japanese words and phrases:

Hai	Yes
Iie	No
O-negai shimasu	Please
Arigato	Thank you
Do itashimashite	You're welcome
Sumimasen	I am sorry

Prominent Japanese:

Basho *Poet*	(1644–1694)
Katsushika Hokusai *Woodblock print artist*	(1760–1849)
Akira Kurosawa *Filmmaker*	(1910–1998)
Meiji *Emperor*	(1852–1912)
Hayao Miyazaki *Anime filmmaker*	(1941–)
Haruki Murakami *Writer*	(1949–)
Ichiro Suzuki *Baseball player*	(1973–)
Banana Yoshimoto *Writer*	(1964–)

To Find Out More

Books

▶ Bjorklund, Ruth. *Aikido*. New York: Marshall Cavendish Benchmark, 2012.

▶ Manga University Culinary Institute. *The Manga Cookbook*. Illus. Chihiro Hattori. Tokyo: Japanime, 2007.

▶ Matthews, Rupert. *Samurai*. New York: Gareth Stevens Publishing, 2016.

Video

▶ *Japanese Drums*. East Grinstead, West Sussex, England: ARC Music, 2010.

▶ *The Japanese Tea Ceremony*. Princeton, NJ: Films for the Humanities & Sciences, 2003.

▶ Visit this Scholastic website for more information on Japan:
www.factsfornow.scholastic.com
Enter the keyword **Japan**

Index

Page numbers in *italics* indicate illustrations.

A

Abe, Shinzo, 66
Academy Awards, 104
Age of Warring States, 45, 64
agriculture
    communities and, 41
    crops, 71–72, 74
    development of, 44, 45
    economy and, 71–72, 74
    farmland, 71
    government and, 42
    Inari (Shinto kami) and, 90
    livestock, 72
    matsuri festivals and, 124–125
    population and, 44
    rice, 70, 71, 124–125
    Shintoism and, 124–125
    Tokugawa shogunate, 47
    tree plantations, 26
aikido (martial art), 120, *121*
Ainu people, 82–83, 84, *84*
airports, 23, 59
Akihito, emperor of Japan, 63, *63*
alpine cypress trees, 28–29
Amaterasu (sun goddess), 41, 64, 90, 95
animal life
    birds, 32–35, *33*, *34*, 107
    climate and, 25, 29
    cranes, 107
    endangered species, 32, 35
    endemic species, 29, 32–33, 35
    geography and, 25
    Hokkaido Island, 30
    Honshu Island, 30
    Inari (kami) and, 90
    Iriomote wildcats, 32
    Japanese green pheasants, 35, *35*
    Japanese macaques, 31–32, *31*
    Japanese red-crowned cranes, 34, *34*
    Kyushu, 30
    livestock, 72
    Okinawa rails, 35
    sables, 30, *30*
    serow, 30
    Shikoku Island, 30
    Shintoism and, 90, 95
    Steller's sea eagles, 33–34, *33*
    tanukis, 31
    Tsushima leopard cats, 32
    whooper swans, 33
    Yaku monkeys, 32
    Yakushima deer, 32
anime, 10, 103–104, *105*, 115, 133
anko (azuki beans), 117
aquaculture, 73
archaeology, 40
archipelago, 15
architecture, 13, 108–109, *109*
art, 10, 42, *42*, 47, 103–104, 106–108, *107*, *108*, 115, 126, 133
artifacts, 40, *40*
artificial intelligence, 77
Ashikaga Takauji, 45
Ashikaga Yoshinori, 45
Aso Crater, *17*
atomic bombs, 56, *57*
Atsuta shrine, 23
automobile industry, 58, *58*, 76
avalanches, 22

B

bamboo, 27–28
baseball, 8, 120, 133
Basho, 100, 133
beech trees, 17

bento boxes, 12
birds, 32–35, *33*, *34*, 107
black-banded sea krait, 36
bluefin tuna, 72, *72*
blue-ringed octopuses, 37
boating, 126
Bon Odori (dance), 101
bowing, 113, *113*
Boy's Day, 125
bridges, *14*, 59
broad-leafed trees, 27
brocade fabric, 105
Buddhism. *See also* religion.
    arrival of, 41
    art and, 106
    Buddha ("Enlightened One"), 42, 91, *91*
    Bushido code and, 55
    Chinese people and, 91
    Enku (monk), 106
    followers of, 96
    funerals, 123–124
    Golden Pavilion, 75, 96, *96*
    government and, 92
    Great Buddha statue, 42, *42*
    introduction of, 91
    Komyo (empress) and, 42
    Korean people and, 91
    language and, 41
    Nanzoin Temple, *91*
    Obon festivals, 12–13, 127, *127*
    Shomu (emperor) and, 42
    spread of, 91
    statues, 42, *42*, *91*, 96
    temples, 96
bullet trains, 11, 79, *79*
Burma, 53
Bushido ("way of the warrior"), 55
Byodo-in Temple, 77

C

camphor tree, 26
capital city. *See* Tokyo.
carp flags, 125, *125*

Charter Oath of Five Principals, 51
cherry blossoms, 29, *29*
Chihira, Aiko, 77
children, 8, 86, *110*, 118, 122, 125
Children's Day, 125
China, 21, 51, 52, *54*, 55, 57, 63
Chinese New Year, 82
Chinese people, 82, *82*, 83, 91
Christianity, 92, 93, 96, 122
chrysanthemums, 29
cities. *See also* Kyoto; Osaka; Tokyo;
   towns; villages.
   Hiroshima, 56, *57*, 107
   Kamaishi, *20*
   Kamakura, 43
   Nagano, 121
   Nagasaki, 56, 96
   Nagoya, 23, 81
   Sapporo, 22, 23, 81, 121
   Yokohama, 23, *49*, 81
citizen-judges, 68
clans, 41
class system, 46, 47
climate, 16, 21–22, 29, 40
clothing, 86, 105–106, *114*–115, 123
communications, 59
cone-bearing trees, 28
Confucianism. *See also* religion.
   Bushido code and, 55
   Confucius, 92, *92*
   temples, 96–97
   Tokugawa shogunate and, 47, 92
conservation, 37, 72
constitution, 50, 57, 61–62, 64
coral reefs, 26, *36*
crafts, 104–106
cranes, 107
cultured pearls, 73, *73*
currency (yen), 44, 48, 77, *77*

D
dance, *84*, 100–101
desserts, 117–118, *118*
Diet, 65–67, 69
district courts, 68

dogu (figurines), *40*
dorayaki (dessert), 117–118
dugongs, 37
Dutch East Indies, 53

E
earthquakes, 19–20, *20*, 59, 78, 109
East China Sea, 15, 18
economy
   agriculture, 71–72, 74
   automobile industry, 58, *58*, 76
   currency (yen), 44, 48, 77, *77*
   employment, *50*, 68, 74–75, *76*, 111
   exports, 23, 104–105
   fishing industry, 72–73
   imports, 53, 59, 72, 73, 74, 77
   logging, 23, 73–74
   manufacturing, *50*, 58–59, *58*, 74,
      76–77
   mining, 74
   sanctions, 54
   service industries, 74–75
   textile industry, *50*, 51, 106
   tourism, 12, 75, *75*
   trade, 47, 48, 49
   United States and, 58
   World War I and, 53
   World War II and, 57, 58–59
Edo, 46, *46*
education, 51, 86, 87, *87*
ekiben (boxed lunch), 11–12
elderly people, 80
elections, 65, 66
electricity, 59, 63, 77–78
ema ("wishing plaques"), 95, *95*
emperors
   Akihito, 63, *63*
   constutiton and, 62
   Hirohito, 54, 56, 63
   Imperial Household Laws and, 62
   Jimmu, 41
   Komei, 49, 50
   Meiji, 50, 51, *51*, 52, 69, 93

   Shomu, 42
empresses
   constitution and, 64
   Imperial Household Laws and, 62
   Koken, 41
   Komyo, 42
   Michiko, 63, *63*
endangered species, 32, 35
endemic species, 29, 32–33, 35
Enku (Buddhist monk), 106
ethnic groups, 81–82
executive branch of government, 62,
   64, 67
exports, 23, 104–105

F
families, 41, 111, 123
fashion design, 115
fast food, *114*, 115
Fillmore, Millard, 48–49
filmmaking industry, 104, *104*, 133, *133*
fishing industry, 72–73
flowers, 21–22, 27, *27*, 28, 29, *29*, 127
foods, 11–12, 71, *72*, *114*, 115–116,
   117–118, 125
forests, *24*, 26, 73–74
France, 52
French Indochina, 53, 55
fue (musical instrument), 101
Fuji-Hakone-Izu National Park, 33
Fukushima nuclear power plant, 59, 78
Fukuzawa, Yukichi, 77
funerals, 123–124

G
gendaimono (Noh plays), 102
geography
   animal life and, 25
   archipelago, 15
   avalanches, 22
   earthquakes, 19–20, *20*, 59, 78, 109
   elevation, 16, 17
   hot springs, 21, *31*
   islands, 11, 15
   lakes, 16, 21, *21*

land area, 15, 16
mountains, 11, 16, *16*, 17
plant life and, 25
rivers, 16, 20–21
tectonic plates, 18, 19
volcanoes, 17, *17*, 18–19
waterfalls, *13*
Germany, 52, 53, 54
Ginza neighborhood, 69
Gion Matsuri festival, 126
Girl's Day, 125
Golden Pavilion, 75, 96, *96*
government. *See also* emperors.
    agriculture and, 42
    Ainu people and, 83
    Buddhism and, 92
    Charter Oath of Five Principals, 51
    chrysanthemums and, 29
    citizen-judges, 68
    conservation and, 26, 34, 37, 72
    constitution, 50, 57, 61–62, 64
    development of, 41
    Diet, 65–67, 69
    district courts, 68
    elections, 65, 66
    executive branch, 62, 64, 67
    House of Representatives, 65–66
    isolation policy, 53
    judicial branch, 62, 67, 68
    laws, 62, 67
    legislative branch, 51, 60, 62, 65–67, 66
    military, 51, 52, *54*, 57
    Minamoto Yoritomo and, 43
    nuclear power and, 78
    parliament building, *60*
    prime ministers, 66, *66*
    San Francisco Peace Treaty, 57
    Sapporo and, 23
    Shintoism and, 93
    shogunate (military rule), 43, 44
    Supreme Court, 68
    taxes, 48

term limits, 66
Treaty of Kanagawa, 49, *49*
Tripartite Act, 54
United States and, 57, 61
women and, 62, 64
The Great Wave (Katsushika Hokusai), 108, *108*
Great Britain, 48, 49–50, 53, 54, 57
Great Buddha statue, 42, *42*

H
Hachijo language, 84
haiku (poetry), 100
hanabiramochi (dessert), 117–118
Hanyu, Yuzuru, 121
health care, 26, 59
Heisei period, 63
Hello Kitty, 115
Himeji Castle, 75
Hinduism, 96, 97
Hinomaru (national flag), 64, *64*
hiragana symbols, 85
Hirohito, emperor of Japan, 54, 56
Hiroshima, 56, *57*, 107
historical maps. *See also* maps.
    Japanese Expansion, *53*
    World War II, *56*
Hitler, Adolf, 54
Hokkaido Island. *See also* islands.
    Ainu people, 82
    animal life, 30
    art, *107*
    climate, 22
    Japanese red-crowned cranes, 34, *34*
    Kushiro Wetlands National Park, 34
    lakes, 21, *21*, *107*
    plant life, 28–29
    population, 15
    railways, 79
    Sapporo Snow Festival, 126, *126*
    whooper swans, 33
Hokusai, Katsushika, 108, *108*, 133
holidays, 124–127
Honshu Island. *See also* islands.

animal life, 30
birds, 34
cities, 23
earthquake, 59
Fuji-Hakone-Izu National Park, 33
lakes, 21
mountains, 17
plant life, 28
population, 15
railways, 79
rivers, 20
tsunami, 59
Tsunoshima Bridge, *14*
volcanoes, 19
hot springs, 21, *31*
House of Councillors, 66
House of Representatives, 65–66
housing, 59, 94, 111–113, *112*
Howl's Moving Castle (film), 104, *105*
humanoid robots, 77
hydroelectric power, 59, 77–78

I
Imperial Household Laws, 62
Imperial Palace, 69
imports, 53, 59, 72, 73, 74, 77
Inari (Shinto kami), 90, 95
Industrial Revolution, 48
insect life, 27, 36
International Whaling Commission, 37
Iriomote-Ishigaki National Park, 18
Iriomote wildcats, 32
Ise Bay, 23
Ise Jingu shrine, 95
Islamic religion, 96, 97
islands. *See also* Hokkaido Island; Honshu Island; Kyushu Island; Okinawa Island.
    Rebun, 25, 29
    Rishiri, 29
    Ryukyu, 26, 83
    Shikoku, 15, 30, 73
    Tsunoshima, *14*
    Tsushima, 15, 32

Yaeyama, 26
Yakushima, 26, 32
Italy, 54

J

Japan Alps, 17
Japanese green pheasant (national
   bird), 35, *35*
Japanese language, 9, 83–84, 85–86, *85*
Japanese macaques, 31–32, *31*
Japanese red-crowned cranes, 34, *34*
Jimmu, emperor of Japan, 41
Jomon culture, 40, *40*
judicial branch of government, 62, 67,
   68
judo (martial art), 120

K

kabuki theater, 102–103
Kamaishi, *20*
Kamakura, 43
kami (clan god), 90, 97
kamikaze pilots, 55
kanji script, 85, 86
Kanto Matsuri festival, 126
karate (martial art), 120
Kasai, Noriaki, 121
kasuri textiles, 106
katakana script, 85
katana swords, 46
katsura trees, 27
Kawabata, Yasunari, 100
kawaii fashion, 115
Kegon Falls, *13*
kendo (martial art), 119–120
Kimigayo (national anthem), 62
kimonos (robes), 105, 114, 123
Koike, Yuriko, 68
Koken, empress of Japan, 41
Kokichi, Mikimoto, 73
Komei, emperor of Japan, 49, 50
Komyo, empress of Japan, 42
konjac flower, 27
Korea, 41, 52, 59
Korean people, 82, 83, 91
koto (musical instrument), 102

Kublai Khan, 45
Kurobe River, 20
Kurosawa, Akira, 104, *104*, 133, *133*
Kushiro Wetlands National Park, 34
Kyoto. *See also* cities.
   as capital city, 42, 45
   climate of, *22*
   Gion Matsuri festival, 126
   Golden Pavilion, 75, 96, *96*
   Oda Nobunaga and, 45
   textile industry, 106
   tourism, 75, *75*
kyudo (archery), 120
Kyushu Island. *See also* islands.
   animal life, 30
   birds, 34
   early settlers, 40
   mountains, 17
   Nanzoin Temple, *91*
   population, 15
   volcanoes, 19

L

Lake Biwa, 21
Lake Hachiro, 16
Lake Mashu, 21, *21*
Lake Tazawa, 16
Lake Toyako, *107*
languages, 9, 41, 83
laws, 62, 67
legislative branch of government, 51,
   60, 62, 65–67, 66
life expectancy, *80*
Lincoln, Abraham, 51
literacy rate, 87
literature, 10, *11*, 47, 99–100, 126, 133
Little League World Series, 8
livestock, 72
Lizard (Banana Yoshimoto), 100
logging, 23, 26, 32, 73–74

M

MacArthur, Douglas, 57, 61
maki sushi (food), 115, *116*
Manchuria, 53
manga, 10, *11*, 12, 103, 104, 115
mangrove swamps, 26
manners, 113, *113*
manufacturing, 50, 58–59, *58*, 74,
   76–77
maps. *See also* historical maps.
   geopolitical, *10*
   population density, *83*
   resources, *72*
   Tokyo, *69*
   topographical, *16*
marine life, 25, *33*, 36, 37, *37*, 40,
   72–73, *72*
Marshall Islands, 53
martial arts, 55, 119–120
matsuri festivals, 12, 97, *97*, 124, 126
Meiji, emperor of Japan, 50, 51, *51*, 52,
   69, 93, 133
memorial services, 124
Micronesia, 53
military, 51, 52, 54, 55, 56, 57
Minamoto Yoritomo, 43, *43*
mining, 74
missionaries, 92
Mitsubishi company, 58
Miyake Island, 33
Miyazaki, Hayao, 104, *105*, 133
mochi (dessert dough), 117
monarchy, 41, 61
Mongols, 44–45, *44*, 64
mosques, 97
Mount Akaishi, 17
Mount Aso, 17, *17*, 19
Mount Fuji, 13, 16, *16*, 17, 21, 79, 108
Mount Hida, 17
Mount Kiso, 17
Mount Ontake, 19
Mount Sakurajima, 19
Murakami, Haruki, 100
music, 102, *103*, 126

N

Nagano, 121
Nagasaki, 56, 96
Nagoya, 23, 81
names, 86, 113, 122, 124
Nanjing, China, 53, *54*
Nanzoin Temple, *91*
national anthem, 62
national baseball team, 120
national bird, 35, *35*
National Diet building, 69
national flag, 64, *64*
national holidays, 124
National Museum of Modern Art, 69
national parks, 13, *13*, 18, 33
national religion, 92
national soccer team, 120
New Year's Day, 125
New Year's Eve, 125
Nikko National Park, 13, *13*, 18
Nintendo company, 104
Nissan company, 58
Nobel Prizes, 100
Noguchi, Hideyo, 77
Noh theater, 98, 102
nori (seaweed), 115
nuclear power, 20, 59, 77, 78

O

obi (sash), 105, 114
Obon festivals, 12–13, 101, 127, *127*
Oda Nobunaga, 45
Oe, Kenzaburo, 100
oil, 52, 53, 55, 59
Okinawa coconut crab, 37
Okinawa Island. *See also* islands.
  birds, 35
  coral reefs, 36
  Okinawa rail, 32, 35
  Okinawan people, 83
  Ryukyuan people, 83
  United States and, 57, 82
Olympic Games, 23, 68, 75, 120–121
omikuji (paper fortunes), 95
onsen (hot springs), 21, *31*
origami (paper art), 107, *107*

Orix Blue Wave (baseball team), 120
Osaka. *See also* cities.
  population of, 23, 81
  port of, 23
  Tenjin Matsuri festival, 126
  tourism, 75

P

Pacific Ocean, 15, 18
pagoda roofs, 109, *109*
paintings, 106–107
Pearl Harbor naval base, 55, 63, 104
pearls, 73, *73*
people
  Ainu, 82–83, 84, *84*
  American ancestry, 82
  ancestors, 81, 82, 127
  bowing, 113, *113*
  children, 8, 86, *110*, 118, 122, 125
  Chinese, 82, *82*, 83, 91
  clans, 41
  class system, 46, 47, 105–106
  clothing, 86, 105–106, 114–115, 123
  commoners, 46
  education, 51, 86, 87, *87*
  elderly, *80*
  employment, 50, 68, 74–75, *76*, 111
  ethnic groups, 81–82
  families, 41, 111, 123
  foods, 71, *114*, 115–116, 125
  funerals, 123–124
  health care, 59
  housing, 59, 94, *112*
  humility, 113
  Jomon culture, 40, *40*
  Korean, 82, 83, 91
  languages, 9, 41, 83
  life expectancy, 80
  literacy rate, 87
  manners, 113, *113*
  memorial services, 124
  Mongols, 44–45, *44*, 64
  names, 86, 113, 122, 124

naming ceremonies, 122
  Okinawan, 83
  population, 11, 26, 81, 83
  prehistoric, 39
  Ryukyuan, 83, 84
  shogun (military commander), 43, *43*
  slurping, 116
  surnames, 86
  voting rights, 65
  weddings, 122–123, *122*
  women, 9–10, 57, 62, 64, 65, 68, *68*, *75*, 102, 113, 114, 115
  Yamato clan, 81
  Yayoi, 89–90
Perry, Matthew, 48–49, *49*
plant life
  alpine cypress trees, 28–29
  bamboo, 27–28
  beech trees, 17
  broad-leafed trees, 27
  camphor tree, 26
  cherry blossoms, 29, *29*
  chrysanthemums, 29
  climate and, 25, 40
  coastlines, 26
  cone-bearing trees, 28
  conservation, 26
  deciduous trees, 28
  flowers, 21–22, *21*, 27, *27*, 28, 29, *29*, 127
  forests, *24*, 26, 73–74
  geography and, 25
  katsura trees, 27
  konjac flower, 27
  mangrove swamps, 26
  mountains, 17
  Ryukyu Islands, 26
  subalpine temperate zones, 28–29
  subarctic temperate zones, 28–29
  temperate zones, 27–28
  trees, 21, 22, 26

variety of, 25
white egret orchid, 27, *27*
Yaeyama Island, 26
Yakushima Island, 26
poetry, 100
population, 11, 26, 44, 81, *83*
port cities, 23
pottery, 104–105
prehistoric people, 39
prime ministers, 64, 66, *66*
printmaking, 108, *108*

R
raccoon dogs. *See* tanukis.
railways, 11–12, 23, 59, *79*
Rebun Island, 25, 29
Records of Wind and Earth, 99
religion. *See also* Buddhism;
    Confucianism; Shintoism.
    Christianity, 92, *93*, 96, 122
    Hinduism, 96, 97
    Islam, 96, 97
    Sikhism, 96, 97
reptilian life, 35–36
rice, *70*, 71, 124–125
Ring of Fire, 18–19
Rishiri Island, 29
Rishiri-Rebun-Sarobetsu National Park,
    18
roadways, *14*, 23, 47
robotics industry, 76–77, *76*
romaji script, 85–86
Roman Catholic Church, 96
Roosevelt, Franklin, 55
Rashomon (film), 104
Russia, 15, 51, 52
Ryukyuan languages, 84
Ryukyuan people, 83, 84
Ryukyu Islands, 26, 83

S
sables, 30, *30*
sake (rice wine), 123
sakuramochi (dessert), 117
Samurai Blue (soccer team), 120
Samurai Japan (baseball team), 120

samurai warriors, 51, 55, 100
    archery and, 120
    Bushido code, 55
    decline of, 45, 48, 51, 55
    Edo, 69
    emergence of, 42–43
    helmets, *38*
    katana swords, 46
    literature, 100
    Mongols and, 45
    Tokugawa shogunate, 47–48
    Tomoe Gozen, 9–10
    topknots, 119
sanctions, 54
San Francisco Peace Treaty, 57
san-san-kudo ritual, 123
Sapporo, 22, 23, 81, 121
Sapporo Snow Festival, 126, *126*
sashimi (food), 116
satoyama (tree plantations), 26
sculpture, 106, *107*
Sea of Japan, 15, 20, 21
Sea of Okhotsk, 15
Seattle Mariners (baseball team), 120
sea turtles, 35–36
Sega company, 104
Seikan Tunnel, 79
serow, 30
service industries, 74–75
Setsubun (holiday), 125–126
shabu-shabu (food), 116
shellfish, 37
shibori textiles, 106
Shikibu, Murasaki, 77, 99
Shikoku Island, 15, 30, 73
Shinano River, 16, 20
Shinjuku area, *12*
shinkansen (bullet trains), 79
Shintoism. *See also* religion.
    agriculture and, 124–125
    altars, 94
    Amaterasu (sun goddess), 41, 64,
        90, 95
    animal life and, 95
    Atsuta shrine, 23

children and, 122
dance and, 100–101
ema ("wishing plaques"), 95, *95*
evil spirits, 90–91, 94
followers of, 96
government and, 93
Inari (kami), 90, 95
Ise Jingu shrine, 95
kami (clan god), 90, 97
kyudo (archery) and, 120
matsuri festivals, 12, 97, *97*, 124, 126
omikuji (paper fortunes), 95
origin of, 89
prayers, 94
shrines, 23, 94–96, *94*, 113, *122*
sumo wrestling and, 119
torii (shrine gates), 94
weddings and, 122, *122*
Yayoi people and, 89
shipping industry, 23
Shiretoko National Park, 18
Shoda, Michiko, 63, *63*
shogun (military commanders)
    Ashikaga Takauji, 45
    Ashikaga Yoshinori, 45
    Minimoto Yoritomo, 43, *43*
    Oda Nobunaga, 45
    Tokugawa clan, 46–47
    Tokugawa Ieyasu, 46
    Toyotomi Hideyoshi, 46
Shomu, emperor of Japan, 42
Sikhism, 96, 97
Sky Tree, 109
snakes, 36
soccer, 120
Sony company, 58–59, 104
South Korea, 15
Soviet Union, 54, 57
Spirited Away (movie), 104
sports, 8, 23, 55, 68, 75, 113, 118–121,
    119, *121*, 133
Steller's sea eagles, 33–34, *33*
storytelling, 99
Summer Olympics, 120–121

sumo wrestling, 55, 119, *119*
Supreme Court, 68
surnames, 86
sushi (food), 115, *116*
Suzuki, Ichiro, 120, 133
sword-hunt program, 46

T

taiko drumming, 102, *103*
The Tale of Genji (Murasaki Shikibu), 99
tanukis, 31
tatami (mats), 112–113, *112*
tea ceremony, 104, 117, *117*
tectonic plates, 19
tempura (food), 115
Tenjin Matsuri festival, 126
textile industry, 50, 51, 106
theater, 98, 102–103
Tojo, Hideki, 54–55
Tokugawa clan, 46–47
Tokugawa Ieyasu, 46
Tokugawa shogunate
    class system, 105–106
    clothing and, 105–106
    Christianity and, 92
    establishment of, 46–47
    Noh theater, 102
    origami and, 107
    tea ceremony, 104
    Tokyo and, 69
Tokyo. *See also* cities.
    architecture, 109
    as capital city, 46
    climate, 16
    as Edo, 46, *46*, 69
    education in, 87
    foods in, *116*
    Ginza neighborhood, 69
    government of, 68, *68*
    Imperial Palace, 69
    map of, 69
    matsuri festival in, 97
    name of, 50
    National Diet building, 69

National Museum of Modern Art, 69
Olympic Games in, 121
origin of, 69
population of, 23, 69, 81
Shinjuku area, *12*
SkyTree, 109
temples in, 88
Tokugawa shogunate and, 69
Tokyo National Museum, 69
tourism in, 11, *12*, 75
train systems in, 78
Ueno Park, 69
Tomoe Gozen, 9–10
Tora! Tora! Tora! (movie), 104
Toshogu Shrine, 13
tourism, 19, 75, *75*
towns. *See also* cities; villages.
    Bon Odori dancers, 101
    matsuri festivals, 124–125
Toyota company, 58
Toyotomi Hideyoshi, 46
trade, 47, 48, 49
transportation, 11, 23, 59, 78–79, *78*, *79*, 111
Treaty of Kanagawa, 49, *49*
Tripartite Act, 54
tsunamis, 19–20, *20*, 59, 63, 78
Tsunoshima Bridge, *14*
Tsunoshima Island, *14*
Tsushima Island, 15, 32
Tsushima leopard cat, 32
turtles, 35–36
typhoons, 22, *44*, 45

U

Ueno Park, 69
Ueshiba, Morihei, 120
United States, 48, 48–49, 51, 53–54, 55, 56, 57, 58, 61, 63, 82, 120

V

video games, 104
villages. *See also* cities; towns.
    Bon Odori dancers, 101

Buddhism in, 96, 101
Edo, 46, *46*
Jomon culture, 40
matsuri festivals, 124–125
trees and, 26
volcanoes, 17, *17*, 18–19
voting rights, *65*

W

Warring States period, 45, 64
wasabi (mustard), 115
waterfalls, *13*
weaving, 105
weddings, 122–123, *122*
whaling, 37, *37*
white egret orchids, 27, *27*
whooper swans, 33
wildlife. *See* animal life; insect life; marine life; plant life; reptilian life.
Winter Olympics, 121
women, 9–10, 57, 62, 64, 65, 68, *68*, 75, 102, 113, 114, 115
World Baseball Classic, 120
World War I, 53
World War II, 54–56, *56*, *57*, 63, 100, 104, 107
written language, 85–86

Y

Yaeyama Island, 26
yagura (Bon Odori structure), 101
Yaku monkeys, 32
Yakushima deer, 32
Yakushima Island, 26, 32
Yamato clan, 81
Yayoi people, 89–90
yen (currency), 44, 48, 77, *77*
Yokohama, 23, 49, 81
yosakoi (dance), 101, *101*
Yoshimoto, Banana, 100, 133
yukata (robe), 114

Meet the Author

RUTH BJORKLUND GREW UP IN RURAL NEW England where she went hiking, rowing, and sailing. She left New England traveled, and eventually settled in Seattle, Washington, where she attended the University of Washington. There, she earned a bachelor's degree in comparative literature and a master's degree in library and information science.

She has been a children's and young adult librarian and has written many books on a wide range of subjects, including states and countries, Native Americans, health, endangered animals, and contemporary issues such as alternative energy and immigration.

Today, Bjorklund lives on Bainbridge Island, a ferry ride away from Seattle. She enjoys kayaking, sailing, camping, and traveling.

Photo Credits